THE COTSWOLD WAY

NATIONAL TRAIL – TWO-WAY TRAIL GUIDE – CHIPPING CAMPDEN TO BATH

By Kev Reynolds,
Lesley and Jonathan Williams

JUNIPER HOUSE, MURLEY MOSS,
OXENHOLME ROAD, KENDAL, CUMBRIA LA9 7RL
www.cicerone.co.uk

Fifth edition 2024
ISBN: 978 1 78631 210 5
Fourth edition 2016
Third edition 2007
Second edition 2005
First edition 1990

Printed in China on responsibly sourced paper on behalf of Latitude Press Ltd.
A catalogue record for this book is available from the British Library.
All photographs are by the authors unless otherwise stated.

1:75k route mapping by Lovell Johns www.lovelljohns.com

Updates to this guide

While every effort is made by our authors to ensure the accuracy of guidebooks as they go to print, changes can occur during the lifetime of an edition. Any updates that we know of for this guide will be on the Cicerone website (www.cicerone.co.uk/1210/updates), so please check before planning your trip. We also advise that you check information about such things as transport, accommodation and shops locally. Even rights of way can be altered over time. We are always grateful for information about any discrepancies between a guidebook and the facts on the ground, sent by email to updates@cicerone.co.uk or by post to Cicerone, Juniper House, Murley Moss, Oxenholme Road, Kendal, LA9 7RL.

Register your book: To sign up to receive free updates, special offers and GPX files where available, create a Cicerone account and register your purchase via the My Account tab at www.cicerone.co.uk.

Front cover: Postlip Hall (Stage 4)

CONTENTS

Acknowledgements

We are grateful to the various Cotswold Way National Trail officers and managers, and for the advice we received from tourist information centres along the way, and other contributions of local expertise and knowledge. The Cotswold Way is one of the true gems of the National Trail network. We would also like to thank the whole Cicerone team for allowing us to moonlight as authors, and for their care and passion in bringing this book together.

ROUTE SUMMARY TABLE

Stage	Start	Finish	Distance (km)	Distance (miles)	Time (hr:min)	Ascent (m)	Descent (m)	Page
1	Chipping Campden	Broadway	9.6	6	2:45	215	265	38
2	Broadway	Stanton	7.0	4	2:00	235	215	44
3	Stanton	Winchcombe	12.3	7¾	3:15	270	280	48
4	Winchcombe	Cleeve Hill	9.2	5¾	3:00	360	200	55
5	Cleeve Hill	Dowdeswell	9.0	5½	2:30	180	330	62
6	Dowdeswell	Birdlip	16.7	10½	4:30	495	350	68
7	Birdlip	Painswick	11.8	7¼	3:30	290	400	75
8	Painswick	Middleyard	15.3	9½	4:15	300	360	82
9	Middleyard	Dursley	10.8	6¾	3:15	410	420	89
10	Dursley	Wotton-under-Edge	12.5	7¾	3:30	295	270	96
11	Wotton-under-Edge	Hawkesbury Upton	11.6	7¼	3:30	390	300	103
12	Hawkesbury Upton	Tormarton	12.1	7½	3:30	260	285	108
13	Tormarton	Cold Ashton	10.4	6½	3:00	240	205	114
14	Cold Ashton	Bath	16.7	10½	4:30	370	540	119
		Totals	**165.0**	**102½**	**47:00**	**4,310**	**4,420**	

The Cotswold Way – North to South

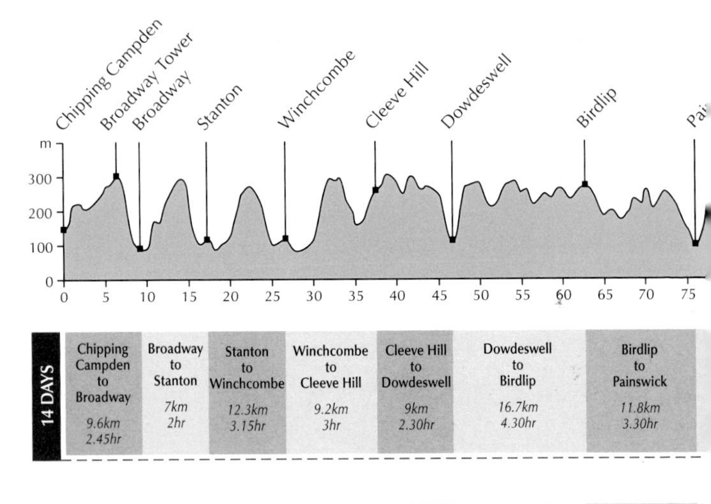

14 DAYS

Chipping Campden to Broadway	Broadway to Stanton	Stanton to Winchcombe	Winchcombe to Cleeve Hill	Cleeve Hill to Dowdeswell	Dowdeswell to Birdlip	Birdlip to Painswick
9.6km 2.45hr	*7km 2hr*	*12.3km 3.15hr*	*9.2km 3hr*	*9km 2.30hr*	*16.7km 4.30hr*	*11.8km 3.30hr*

10 DAYS

Chipping Campden to Stanton	Stanton to Winchcombe	Winchcombe to Dowdeswell	Dowdeswell to Birdlip	Birdlip to Painswick
16.6km 4.45hr	*12.3km 3.15hr*	*18.2km 5.30hr*	*16.7km 4.30hr*	*11.8km 3.30hr*

8 DAYS

Chipping Campden to Stanton	Stanton to Winchcombe	Winchcombe to Dowdeswell	Dowdeswell to Birdlip	Birdl to Middle
16.6km 4.45hr	*12.3km 3.15hr*	*18.2km 5.30hr*	*16.7km 4.30hr*	*27.1k 7.45*

7 DAYS

Chipping Campden to Stanton	Stanton to Cleeve Hill	Cleeve Hill to Birdlip	Birdl to Middle
16.6km 4.45hr	*21.5km 6.15hr*	*25.7km 7hr*	*27.1k 7.45*

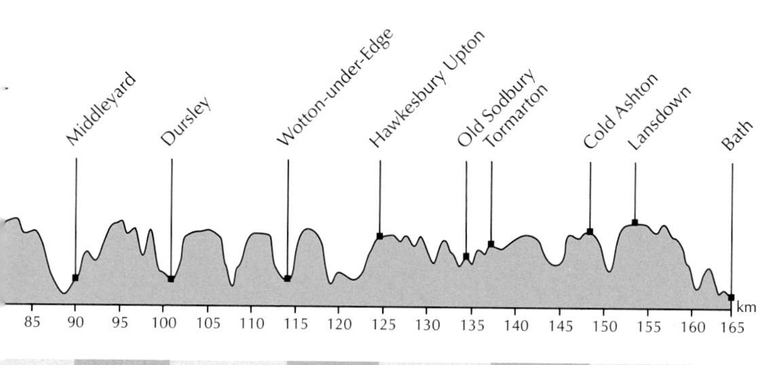

ıswick to dleyard .3km 15hr	Middleyard to Dursley 10.8km 3.15hr	Dursley to Wotton-under-Edge 12.5km 3.30hr	Wotton-under-Edge to Hawkesbury Upton 11.6km 3.30hr	Hawkesbury Upton to Tormarton 12.1km 3.30hr	Tormarton to Cold Ashton 10.4km 3hr	Cold Ashton to Bath 16.7km 4.30hr

AVERAGE DAY – 11.8km / 3hr 30min

ıswick to dleyard .3km 15hr	Middleyard to Wotton-under-Edge 23.3km 6.45hr	Wotton-under-Edge to Old Sodbury 19.8km 5.50hr	Old Sodbury to Lansdown 19km 5.30hr	Lansdown to Bath 12km 3.10hr

AVERAGE DAY – 16.5km / 4hr 45min

Middleyard to Wotton-under-Edge 23.3km 6.45hr	Wotton-under-Edge to Tormarton 23.7km 7hr	Tormarton to Bath 27.1km 7.30hr

AVERAGE DAY – 20.6km / 6hr

Middleyard to Wotton-under-Edge 23.3km 6.45hr	Wotton-under-Edge to Tormarton 23.7km 7hr	Tormarton to Bath 27.1km 7.30hr

AVERAGE DAY – 23.6km / 6hr 45min

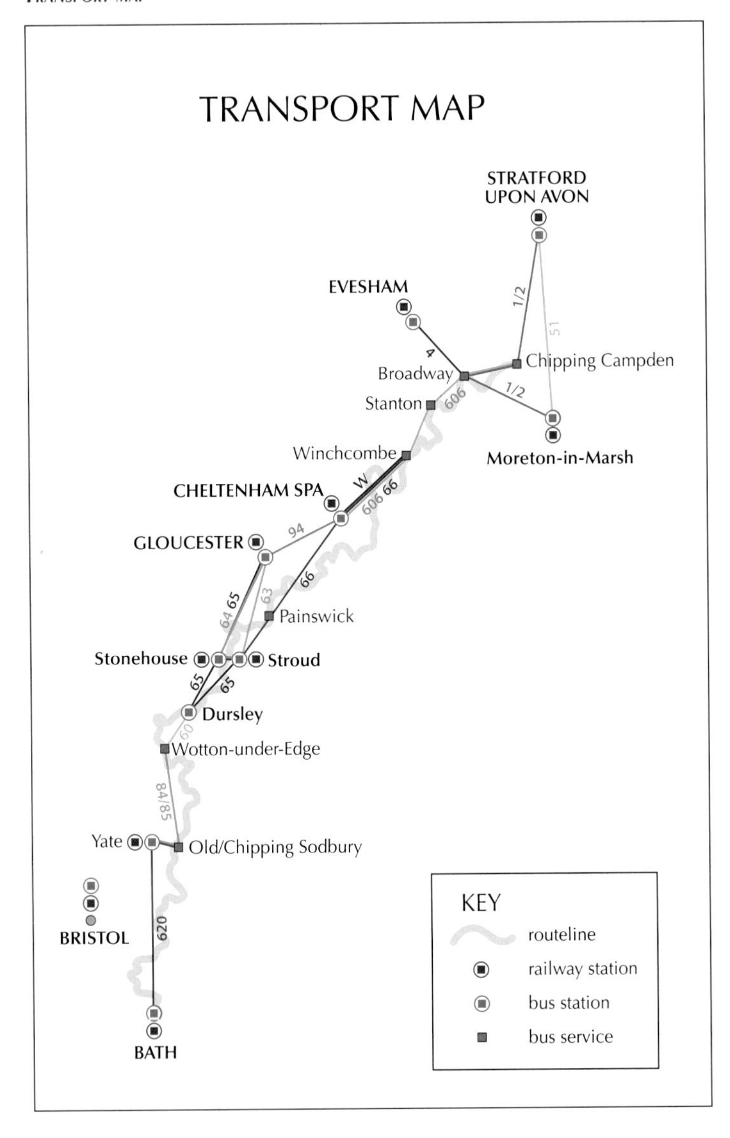
TRANSPORT MAP
STRATFORD UPON AVON
EVESHAM
1/2
51
4
Broadway
Chipping Campden
1/2
Stanton
606
Moreton-in-Marsh
Winchcombe
W
66
606
CHELTENHAM SPA
94
GLOUCESTER
66
64
65
63
Painswick
Stonehouse
Stroud
65
65
Dursley
60
Wotton-under-Edge
84/85
Yate
Old/Chipping Sodbury
BRISTOL
620
BATH
KEY
routeline
railway station
bus station
bus service

Symbols on the route maps

route
alternative route
direction of route
start point
finish point
station/railway line
bus service
railway station
accommodation
cash
refreshments
shopping
tourist information
abbey
camping
building
other feature

SCALE: 1:75,000

0 kilometres 1
0 miles 1

Contour lines are drawn at 50m intervals and labelled at 100m intervals.

Route map relief
400m
300m
200m
100m

GPX files for all routes can be downloaded free at www.cicerone.co.uk/1210/GPX.

Features on the overview map

County/Unitary boundary
National boundary
Urban area
Area of Outstanding Natural Beauty eg *Malvern Hills*

Overview map relief
400m
200m
75m
0m

See 1:25,000 map booklet for the key to the 1:25,000 maps

STAGE FACILITIES PLANNER

Stage	Finish	Distance (km)	Cumulative distance (km)	Time (hr:min)
	Chipping Campden			
1	Broadway	9.6	9.6	2:45
2	Stanton	7.0	16.6	2:00
3	Stanway	2.4	19.0	0:40
3	Wood Stanway	1.2	20.2	0:20
3	North Farmcote	2.3	24.2	0:30
3	Hayles Fruit Farm	0.9	25.1	0:15
3	Winchcombe	3.8	28.9	1:00
4	Postlip Farm	7.4	36.3	2:30
4	Cleeve Hill	1.8	38.1	0:30
5	Dowdeswell	9.0	47.1	2:30
6	Seven Springs	4.6	51.7	1:20
6	National Star College	5.5	57.2	1:30
6	Crickley Hill	3.0	60.2	0:40
6	Birdlip	3.6	63.8	1:00
7	Cranham Corner	7.4	71.2	2:15
7	Painswick	4.4	75.6	1:15
8	Edgemoor Inn	2.2	77.8	0:45
8	King's Stanley/Middleyard	13.1	90.9	3:30
9	Nympsfield	3.8	94.7	1:15
9	Dursley	7.0	101.7	2:00
10	North Nibley	7.8	109.5	2:15
10	Wotton-under-Edge	4.7	114.2	1:15
11	Alderley	5.9	120.1	1:45
11	Lower Kilcott	2.7	122.8	0:45
11	Hawkesbury Upton	3.0	125.8	1:00
12	Little Sodbury	5.5	131.3	1:30
12	Old Sodbury	2.8	134.1	0:50
12	Tormarton	3.8	137.9	1:10
13	Pennsylvania	9.3	147.2	2:45
13	Cold Ashton	1.1	148.3	0:15
14	Lansdown	4.7	153.0	1:20
14	Bath	12.0	165.0	3:10

campsite hotel/B&B/guesthouse refreshments grocery shop

bus service train station information ATM

Facilities

Broadway Tower (Stage 1)

INTRODUCTION

Looking south from Randwick, the villages around Stroud are clearly seen (Stage 7)

Curious to know how our most recent walk of the Cotswold Way went, several people enquired about our impressions and experiences within days of our arriving home. We had walked the route in both directions during late April and early May, although Lesley had also walked the route some 10 years previously, during a very warm week in September. Keen to understand and really get to know the trail intimately, we were determined to give everything as much time as it deserved. Our impressions were as varied as the trail itself.

Man has lived in close harmony with the landscape of the Cotswolds for thousands of years. We were fascinated by how life must have been for Neolithic man as we visited Belas Knap, and we wondered in some awe at the scale of the earthworks surrounding the many Iron Age hill forts. We enjoyed deciding which villages and towns felt like living museums, and which felt more vibrant and comfortable with themselves. The friendly and helpful locals were always ready to offer advice and suggestions, and we enjoyed many cakes and mugs of tea along the way.

We marvelled at the progress of the growing crops in vast upland fields – in just two or three weeks these changed dramatically – and at the calves and lambs playing in fields and meadows, the heritage and enormous wealth created by the wool industry visible everywhere. We spent hours striding out across wide open downland with massive views to Wales and the Severn estuary. We walked through beech woods, marvelling at the shafts of sunlight streaming through the fresh green leaves, the woodland floor turned cobalt with bluebells.

There were some more overcast days, torrential cloudbursts, cold winds sapping energy, and then there was mud – mainly soft and squelchy, but sometimes slippery clay that clung to our boots, adding time and energy to a day's walking.

Would we walk it again next week, or next year? Yes, definitely. It's a trail that lures you back with its treasures and variety.

THE COTSWOLD WAY

This is a route that, if time allows, is to be enjoyed in an unhurried way. There are so many places of interest nearby – Neolithic hill forts and burial chambers, castles, churches and ruined abbeys, battlefields and museums in historic market towns. The route passes through over 14 nature reserves and some of Europe's best and most extensive beech woods, bright with fresh green leaves in spring, and of incredible beauty in autumn when leaves turn to multiple shades of gold, amber and copper. Carpets of bluebells and ramsons (wild garlic) cover vast areas of the woodland floor in spring. Wildflowers – including rare orchids – are abundant in the protected upland areas, while butterflies thrive around several protected areas.

And then there are the views – vast stretches of the Severn Valley punctuated by outlying hills, with the Malvern Hills and Welsh mountains forming a backdrop. High points of between 200–300m on the scarp edge contrast with paths and tracks through sheltered woodlands filled with birdsong. Some slopes are gentle inclines, while others rise steeply in sunken lanes; but for all that there is never more than around 200m to climb or descend at any one time. The earth is fragile – grassy uplands are well drained, but deep in the woodlands dampness remains even during dry spells, and occasionally stretches of path can become mired in a muddy soup, especially when the route is shared with a bridleway, making progress slow and slippery.

The route meanders along the Cotswold 'edges' and at times appears convoluted, but it is always deliberate, as if keen to ensure that as many highlights as possible are visited and explored to reveal the very essence of the Cotswolds, the spirit of the region.

The journey is one to enjoy. At 102 miles (165km) – between Chipping Campden and Bath – it's long enough to feel meaningful, and the daily ascent and descent

A quiet morning In Broadway (Stage 1)

(sometimes more than once) of the escarpment, or 'edge', between the charming villages below can be a challenge for some, and yet is manageable for walkers of most abilities.

OUTLINE OF THE ROUTE

Barely more than half an hour after leaving Chipping Campden you reach the escarpment for the first time at Dover's Hill, to enjoy far-reaching views across the Severn valley towards the distant mountains of Wales. There will be similar views repeated as you make your journey south (or northwards if starting in Bath). Passing Broadway Tower, a grassy descent leads directly into Broadway, one of the more picturesque small towns.

The old villages of Stanton, Stanway and Wood Stanway follow as you climb and descend off the escarpment, passing the ruins of Hailes Abbey to reach Winchcombe, a bustling little market town with Sudeley Castle nearby.

From Winchcombe, climb again to reach Belas Knap, an impressive Neolithic long barrow, then through the first of many magnificent woods to reach Cleeve Common, the highest point on the Cotswold Way and the site of one of many Iron Age hill forts on the route.

Elevated views across the Severn valley to the Malvern Hills, Black Mountains and Bannau Brycheiniog (Brecon Beacons) from Leckhampton Hill and the ancient Neolithic site on Crickley Hill are exhilarating. After Birdlip the trail passes through protected beech woods to reach elegant Painswick, close to halfway to Bath, then through more woods and to more fine vantage points before dropping into the Stroud Valley.

The escarpment provides many fine views and the sites of more promontory hill forts on the way to the thriving yet traditional town of Dursley. Then the route continues over to Wotton-under-Edge via North Nibley, with the impressive monument to Tyndale on Nibley Knoll.

Entering more mellow landscapes, the trail passes the pretty mill villages of the Kilcott Valley to Hawkesbury Upton, skirting just above 12th-century Horton Court, then through the Sodbury villages and large hill fort. Manicured Dodington Park is crossed to reach Tormarton, then the ancient deer park and house of Dyrham.

The escarpment is visited for the final time at Lansdown, passing the 1643 battlefield, an Iron Age hill fort and a racecourse before the final descent into the elegant streets of Bath to reach the abbey and Roman Baths.

Plaques mark the start in Chipping Campden and finish at Bath Abbey

TRAIL BACKGROUND

In the 1950s, plans for the Cotswold Way were developed by the Gloucestershire County Council, and the trail was launched in May 1970 to celebrate European Conservation Year. Enthusiastic volunteers from the Cotswold Wardens and the Ramblers comprehensively waymarked the route over the course of the next few years, then in 2007 the Cotswold Way became recognised as a National Trail, benefiting from additional funding and conservation powers, along with new waymarking displaying the iconic acorn motif used for all National Trails.

The Cotswold Way Association is a charity which works to improve the trail, working alongside the National Trail Wardens. Improvements and changes to the trail are posted on the National Trail website (www.nationaltrail.co.uk/cotswold-way).

Should you find any major changes not shown on the National Trail website or in this guidebook, we would be grateful if you could notify Cicerone using the Contact form on www.cicerone.co.uk/contact. Updates will be posted on the Cicerone website, and if permanent, will be included in future printed guides.

The National Trail website (www.nationaltrail.co.uk/cotswold-way) also suggests a series of circular day walks to cover the trail, which are particularly useful for those based locally.

PLANNING YOUR TRIP

Cider and food at Dunkertons just off route at Dowdeswell are very welcome (Stage 5)

At 165km (102 miles), the CW can be walked in less than a week or extended over nearly two weeks. This guide has broken the route into 14 stages, based around locations with accommodation and natural break points, but almost all walkers will want to combine stages as they develop their own schedules for a walk of around 7–10 days. Speed merchants can manage the trail in fewer days but will miss out on the many features along the trail.

Preference will be important in determining plans. Perhaps visiting houses, monuments, churches and Neolithic sites along the trail is a priority. Some may want to study the wildflowers, fungi and natural wonders on the way. There is certainly plenty to see and it's a trail best not rushed. As a guide, most walkers will average about 4km (2½ miles) per hour actual walking time, although in hot or more challenging conditions progress might be slower.

The Stage facilities planner provided shows where it might be possible to stop for snacks or other facilities as well as accommodation along the route, and this can help with planning each day.

The deeply sunken lane climbed on the way to the Tyndale Monument from North Nibley (Stage 10)

WHEN TO GO

Although seasonal weather patterns are generally reliable, it is unlikely that you will have stable weather for the entirety of your trek on the Cotswold Way. There are many things to consider!

In spring, roughly between April to June, there is usually less rainfall, and the abundance of wildflowers, bright fresh leaves and spring colours is a delight. Most facilities and attractions will be open; however, accommodation in late April/early May is expensive, and is often under pressure due to a number of festivals, including the Badminton Horse Trails.

Summer is the most popular time for walking the route, but once again accommodation will be under pressure from other tourists in the area, and single-night stays are less likely to be available. Temperatures for walking may be occasionally hot and uncomfortable.

Autumn can be both dry and pleasantly warm, with the bonus of the extensive beech woods – vibrant in yellow and gold autumn colours. Some of the facilities and attractions will close during this period, but there will also be fewer crowds competing for accommodation.

In winter there may be more challenges: wet and cold weather, short daylight hours, reduced options for accommodation and difficult conditions underfoot, although for strong walkers a week of dry, frosty weather would be magical.

WHICH DIRECTION?

The Cotswold Way has been waymarked in a way that makes the route equally clear in both directions. If walking north from Bath, you will probably have the prevailing wind and the sun on your back, and the more dramatic scenery, which builds as you progress towards Chipping Campden. But most people walk in a southerly direction, with Bath as a more significant finish point, with good onward transport by rail. While this guide describes the route in both directions, emphasis is placed on the north to south description, and items of interest, maps and route profiles are only included for the southbound description.

Transport is also a consideration, as travelling to Chipping Campden from most areas will be a combination of train and local bus or taxi, which might allow you to arrive in Chipping Campden sometime in early afternoon. The first short stage from Chipping Campden to Broadway is suggested to provide an opportunity for an easy half-day introduction to the route. Similarly, if walking northbound, there is accommodation at Lansdown for a short first day.

While Chipping Campden has much to offer with its charming buildings, it is a small town and it is likely that after a few hours you will be keen to either start the trail, or to start your homeward journey. By contrast, the World Heritage City of Bath has much to offer and explore, so allowing a day or two here is recommended. Many of the city's elegant buildings were built from the 15th century onwards, but it is the city's Roman history that makes it truly fascinating. In Roman times, Bath was known as Aquae Sulis. Visiting the excavated Roman Baths is a very worthwhile excursion, providing insights into the development of the town and surrounding region in Roman times. (For more information about Bath see Stage 14.)

The finish at Bath Abbey (Stage 14)

ACCOMMODATION

Accommodation is likely to be a crucial factor, especially in high summer. Booking well ahead is recommended, since accommodation options along the trail – while reasonable – are somewhat scarce, and the CW walker must compete with other visitors. Sometimes it will be necessary to leave the trail to access accommodation, either via a short walk, bus ride or even taxi. Only in a few places is there good accommodation between the stage ends.

Appendix B lists most of the more affordable accommodation within 1.5km of the trail. The National Trail website www.nationaltrail.co.uk/cotswold-way also has a useful list

The Somerset Monument at Hawkesbury Upton (Stage 11)

of accommodation; however, some listings may be a fair distance from the trail.

Camping

Camping is limited along the trail, and wild camping is not permitted at any point along the route. There are a few official campsites – including at Hayles Fruit Farm – with a number of seasonal facilities, including pitches at glamping sites. A list of known sites is in Appendix B.

STAGE PLANNING

The route has been split into 14 stages, averaging approximately 12km (7½ miles) each and based around the availability of accommodation. Given the need to book this well ahead, the CW walker's stage plan will need to take account of accommodation as well as stage length.

- Southbound walkers starting from Chipping Campden can combine the first two stages or, if they arrive in good time, walk the 2hr 45min route to Broadway.
- Accommodation near Dowdeswell is in a hotel in Charlton Kings, 15min walk towards Cheltenham, and there is ample (usually expensive) accommodation in Cheltenham.
- Think carefully about whether to combine the 17km stage into Birdlip with either the previous or following stage, as this will make for a very long day.
- Accommodation near Stroud, where the trail splits, is often off route.
- The last four stages of the walk tend to be easier walking, so taking two days from Wotton-under-Edge to Bath is very feasible.
- Northbound walkers from Bath may wish to start with a shorter stage to Lansdown Golf Course or Cold Ashton.

SUGGESTED SCHEDULES

The schedules in the Alternate schedule planner have been compiled as illustrative staging for tackling the Cotswold Way. There are some long days on the 7-day schedule, while schedules for 8 and 10 days will give some much shorter stages for inspecting sites and recovery. It's arguably a walk to spend as long as possible on, not a trail to rush along – there are no prizes for speed!

GUIDED AND SELF-GUIDED HOLIDAYS AND BAGGAGE TRANSFER

You can of course leave much or all the planning to a walking holiday company. Many companies will provide options so that you can choose how many days you want to take to walk the trail, and the holiday company will arrange accommodation along the route. Baggage transfer can be arranged both through a holiday company or directly with a baggage transfer company. The trail is very well waymarked, so self-guided walking is recommended unless walking in a guided group is your preference. See Appendix A for suggestions.

TRANSPORT TO AND AROUND THE COTSWOLDS

The hilly nature of the Cotswolds means that much of the public transport network is by bus, although a number of rail services connect some of the major towns. A map showing the main transport options available at the time of writing is at the beginning of the book.

Train services connect London with Bath (in 90min), as well as Stroud, Cheltenham, Moreton-in-Marsh and Evesham. Stratford-upon-Avon is served by rail from Birmingham. The Birmingham to Bristol line gives an opportunity to reach sections of the Cotswold Way from stations at Ashchurch, Cheltenham, Gloucester, and Cam and Dursley. At the time of writing, bus services connect Chipping Campden with the rail network at Evesham, Stratford-upon-Avon and Moreton-in-Marsh. National Express coaches serve Bath and Cheltenham.

Bus routes into and along the Cotswolds are operated by several companies. Unfortunately, it is not possible to provide accurate information in this guide, as operators are permitted to change or cancel services, provided they give six weeks' notice to the county councils, and they often do so. For national bus timetable information visit www.traveline.info. The website https://bustimes.org has a good search function and seems to be one of the more reliable and useful sources of information on bus times and routes.

EQUIPMENT AND OTHER PRACTICALITIES

Clothing

Take clothing and equipment appropriate for the season. Waterproofs should be carried at all times of the year. Choose comfortable, well-fitting boots. Walking poles are recommended, as they provide additional stability when negotiating steep or muddy sections of the trail. Always ensure you have a few snacks with you and plenty of water, especially in hot summer months. A first-aid kit to deal with minor injuries and blisters is recommended. Carry a map (or the map booklet provided), the guidebook and a compass. Even when carrying all your clothing and equipment, you should be able to keep your pack fairly light, under say 6kg. In addition to the items already mentioned, you shouldn't need much more than two base layers, a fleece, underwear and two pairs of walking socks (plus a pair or two for the evenings), as well as a sun hat, sun cream and normal toiletries/medication. It should be possible to wash and dry clothing overnight.

The outlines of the old hill fort on Cleeve Hill (Stage 5)

Mobile phones and signal

A mobile phone is almost essential for day-to-day checks on the weather, mapping, transport or accommodation; however, mobile signal is not always reliable, and wi-fi in accommodation – although usually available – may be slow. Try to ensure any mapping or other data-rich information is downloaded while you have good signal.

Apps

Mobile phone apps can provide a wealth of information. For general search, Google maps will provide information on public transport, accommodation, location, and everything else you can think of! You may find it useful to use a mapping app, especially one displaying OS mapping – OS® maps, and OutdoorActive are both popular. Accommodation is probably best searched on Google, Booking.com, Airbnb and other similar websites. Your preferred weather forecast app will be useful too. If using GPS tracks, make sure you are happy with how they have downloaded before you leave.

Maps

A map booklet using 1:25,000 OS mapping is provided; however, other sheet maps covering the Cotswold Way are available, as is OS mapping on mobile phone apps. To cover the entire route, you will need OS Landranger 1:50,000 sheets numbers 151, 162, 163 and 172, or – for more detail – OS Explorer 1:25,000 OL45, 155, 167, 168 and 179. Ordnance survey maps come with a free digital download option, for use on multiple devices and the OS maps app. A Harvey map at 1:40,000 sheet XT40 is also available showing the entire route.

ON THE TRAIL

CW finger post

USING THIS GUIDE

Each stage of this route description begins with a summary of the start and finish points, distance, approximate time needed for the walk, ascent and descent, and an indication of where facilities and accommodation can be found. Distances are quoted in kilometres and (miles). Features that appear on the stage maps are highlighted in bold in the route descriptions, in order to help you plot your way across the maps, and lots of information is given about points of historical, geological or general interest that are passed along the way.

Stage maps and profiles are designed to help with visualising and planning. As mentioned earlier, the further ahead you can make plans and book accommodation the better. If you are not completely trail fit, it might be worth spending the first few days doing shorter stages while you get accustomed to the trail.

WAYMARKING ON THE ROUTE

The route uses established footpaths (with direction arrows on a yellow background) and bridleways (similar, with a blue background). There are sometimes various crossing paths, but the Way itself is clearly marked with the National Trail acorn symbol.

When going through towns and villages other signs may be used: finger posts, signs on lamp posts, curb stones and other street furniture. Some, such as those in the Primrose Hill area in Bath, are even found unusually high up!

HEALTH, SAFETY AND EMERGENCIES

While there are a number of busy roads requiring care when crossing, especially towards the southern end of the route, natural hazards are unlikely; however, be especially careful when descending steep slopes

The folly above Little Sodbury (Stage 12)

during or after rain when paths can become very slippery – trekking poles can be a great help with this and can reduce the chance of knee strain. Prolonged rain can sap energy. If caught out in a thunderstorm, take shelter away from high, open ground, but not beneath isolated trees.

When out for much of the day during hot summer weather, sunburn might be an issue, so wearing a sunhat and applying sunscreen is advised. There may be few places on some stages where water can be refilled, so ensure you have an adequate supply to stay hydrated.

There is usually nothing to worry about when crossing the occasional field with cattle grazing, although if you're walking with a dog, be especially careful, since cows may be nervous and may react out of character. Keep your dog under close control, but should you be threatened, let the dog run free and the cows will chase after it – not you.

In summer, it is possible that you might encounter an adder basking in the sunshine, especially on the grassy downland. They are only likely to be a threat if disturbed, so pass with caution. Dog owners are advised to keep their pets on a lead to prevent the possibility of an attack. There are signs for adders on Cleeve Common, although we have not seen any.

The best way to avoid blisters is not to allow them to develop! Make sure you are wearing comfortable, tried and tested boots, and wash socks daily. If you feel any discomfort, stop and apply tape, moleskin or Compeed to the irritated area before a blister can develop.

Ticks

Ticks, which can cause Lyme Disease, inhabit long grass, bracken and shrubs and can attach themselves to you as you walk past, especially if skin is exposed. The tick injects a toxin to anaesthetise the bite, so you will not always notice until later in the day. Check pressure points where clothing presses against the skin each evening – especially the back of the knee, armpits and groin. To remove a tick, ideally use tweezers to grasp as close to the skin as possible and pull the body steadily outwards, without twisting or jerking. The buried head should come away cleanly, then cleanse the area with disinfectant. If you feel ill or develop a fever a few days later, consult a doctor.

THE COUNTRY CODE

- Enjoy the countryside and respect its life and work.
- Guard against all risks of fire.
- Fasten all gates.
- Keep dogs under close control.
- Keep to public paths across farmland.
- Use gates and stiles to cross fences, hedges and walls.
- Leave livestock, crops and machinery alone.
- Take litter home.
- Help to keep all water clean.
- Protect wildlife, plants and trees.
- Take special care on country roads.
- Make no unnecessary noise.

Look up for CW signage in Bath

ABOUT THE COTSWOLDS

An old quarry shows the colour of the local Cotswold stone

The Cotswolds are part of an extensive belt of limestone which runs diagonally across England from Dorset's Jurassic Coast to the White Peak. The Cotswolds are the highest and broadest part, with a steep and distinct scarp edge dropping to the Severn Plain in the west, and gently sloping land towards the Thames Valley and Oxfordshire Plain in the east.

Much of the route passes through the Cotswolds Area of Outstanding Natural Beauty and numerous wildlife conservation reserves, as well as visiting the considerable beauty and charm of the historic towns and villages along the way. Man's occupation in the area has a very long history, with mounds and barrows scattered along the way and numerous impressive hill forts perched on the steep scarp slope, which would have provided a natural defence line and good visibility to spot approaching danger.

Roman villas are scattered through the area, while the sheep rearing of the Middle Ages made the Cotswolds renowned throughout Europe for its fine fleeces. More recently, the area has accommodated substantial houses and a range of monuments.

GEOLOGY

The Cotswolds were formed between 210 and 140 million years ago. They are made up of three different types of Jurassic rock and extend in a broad band for nearly 60 miles. The Lower Jurassic rocks – collectively called the Lias Group – consist of clays, sand and silt, while above this layer the Middle Jurassic rocks consist of the Inferior Oolitic and Great Oolitic Groups. Oolitic indicates an accumulation of rounded rocks made up into concentric layers.

All these deposits were almost exclusively formed under mainly warm tropical seas – the Lias Group as a result of materials being transported by rivers and the wind, and the Middle Jurassic from deposits of calcium carbonate and the accumulation of chemicals from dead organisms, including fossils. All these layers were then compressed and transported northwards over the last 150–200 million years by the movement of tectonic plates to their current location. They tilted slightly, dropping towards the east, leaving the scarp edge to the west.

The thickest and most complete Inferior Oolitic rocks can be seen on Cleeve Common and are designated as a Site of Special Scientific Interest. These are the soft yellow sandy limestones which gradually become harder higher up. You can particularly notice these on the precipitous scarp slope of Cleeve Common, the outcrop of Castle Rock demonstrating the relative resistance of these harder rocks. The thick beds of fine-grained Oolitic limestone of the 'Birdlip Limestone Formation' are used for high-quality building stone.

Natural weathering and water erosion from the numerous springs and streams has gradually worn into the scarp edge, weakening it to form the numerous projecting spurs and bays, with more resistant outlying hills such as Cam Long Down suggesting the escarpment might once have extended considerably further west.

Above the Inferior Oolitic rocks lie the Great Oolitic Group. These are very varied rocks and formations, including fuller's earth, a thick bed of clay that contains a mineral used to remove the grease from fleeces, which contributed to the huge success of the wool trade in the area during the Middle Ages.

By the end of the Ice Age, around 10,000 years ago, vegetation sprang up in the fertile glacial deposits. Woodland was cleared during Neolithic times to provide space for primitive agriculture. By the Middle Ages huge areas were given over to sheep pasture for the thriving wool trade, but since then there has been a more varied mix of land use, with most recent developments focusing more on conservation and the management of unique natural woodlands.

NATURE AND WILDLIFE

The entire area is covered by the Cotswolds Area of Outstanding Natural Beauty, within which there are numerous nature reserves, including the Cotswold Commons and Beechwoods National Nature Reserve

Spring bluebells in Buckholt Wood (Stage 7)

(NNR), the largest nature reserve in the Cotswolds. It is largely made up of a chain of beechwoods and limestone grasslands around the upper slopes of the Painswick Valley. The beechwoods are also protected as a European Special Area of Conservation because they are rich in rare wildlife, although the exact future of this status is unclear.

The Cotswold Way passes directly through the following nature reserves (in order from north to south):

- Dover's Hill Nature Reserve – a natural amphitheatre of woodland and grass meadows
- Cleeve Hill Common Nature Reserve – a Grade 1 Site of Special Scientific Interest for its geology, habitats and botany, as well as archaeological sites and Scheduled Monuments (see Stage 3 for more information)
- Arle Grove Nature Reserve near Dowdeswell – an ancient woodland rich in rare species of plants and animals
- Rough Bank Butterfly Conservation Reserve – a flower-rich grassland, ideal for butterflies and moths, including six species of blue butterfly
- Dowdeswell Woods Nature Reserve – an 80-hectare (200-acre) woodland, most of which is classified as ancient woodland
- Witcombe Wood National Forest – deciduous woodland
- Cooper's Hill Nature Reserve – 134 acres of protected ancient beech woodland
- Rough Park – ancient beechwoods
- Cranham Common – ancient beechwoods

- Buckholt Woods – woodland, especially noted for over 780 species of fungi
- Pope's Wood – mixed woodland on the edge of the escarpment
- Rudge Hill (Edge Common) Nature Reserve – woodland and unimproved grassland supporting butterflies, including the rare Duke of Burgundy fritillary, wildflowers and orchids
- Cam Long Down and Cam Peak Nature Reserves – unimproved grassland, woods and bluebells

The open expanses of grassland on the high common lands is home to a variety of plants including yellow rattle, knapweed, harebell and wild thyme. Cleeve Common is a Grade 1 Site of Special Scientific Interest supporting over 150 species of herbs and grasses. In early summer, orchids thrive on the uncultivated land, including pyramidal, greater butterfly, common spotted, and early purple varieties.

These plants in turn attract many insects, including butterflies, for which the area is particularly well known. Grassland varieties include chalkhill blue, Adonis blue, small blue, dingy skipper, and the rare Duke of Burgundy fritillary.

Under the trees, the woodland floors are often covered with vast carpets of bluebells and ramsons, as well as hellebores, bird's nest orchids, wood barley and wintergreen. The more open areas are alive with butterflies in summer, while hedgerows support a variety of grasses, vetch, wild clematis, gorse and hawthorn, creating a wonderful patchwork of colour in spring and summer.

Rare spiders and snails may be seen in the ancient woodlands, along with larger animals, such as squirrels, rabbits, hares, foxes, badgers and deer – especially the ancient herd of fallow deer at Dyrham Park.

The skies above the escarpment are filled with birds both day and night, including skylarks, tree pipits, pheasants, kestrels, buzzards and tawny owls. The sound of the lesser-spotted woodpecker in spring and early summer hammering in the trees is a true delight.

THE EARLY OCCUPATION OF THE COTSWOLDS

'Man in the landscape' could well be the walk's theme. Man has lived in harmony with nature for a long time here, using as a basic building material the very substance of the land, exhibiting a rare degree of artistry in the moulding of wall, doorway and crooked roof, until even the villages themselves appeared to be an extension of that land, an integral part of the landscape.

Instead of shunning habitation, as do many other long-distance paths, the Cotswold Way actively seeks out the villages and towns that are among the loveliest features of the region, along with the many impressive features left behind by

Belas Knap Burial Mound (Stage 4)

man's ancient ancestors, who worked and shaped the landscape for over 5000 years.

A great many ancient sites are passed which lie directly on the route, the main ones are:

Stage	Name	Notes
2	Shenberrow Hill	Iron Age hill fort
3	Beckbury Hill Fort	Iron Age hill fort
4	Belas Knap	Long barrow dating from 3000BC
5	Cleeve Cloud Hill Fort	Iron Age hill fort
6	Leckhampton Hill	Iron Age hill fort
6	Crickley Hill	Multiple phases of occupation from 4000BC
7	Painswick Beacon	Iron Age hill fort
8	Haresfield Beacon	Iron Age hill fort
9	Nympsfield Long Barrow	Long barrow dating from 2800BC
9	Hetty Pegler's Tump	Neolithic long barrow
9	Uley Bury	Very large (30-acre) Iron Age hill fort
11	Horton Fort	Iron Age hill fort
11	Sodbury Hill Fort	Large (11-acre) Iron Age hill fort
13	Little Down Fort	Iron Age hill fort

To provide context to this impressive list, the brief history below outlines the phases of early occupation in the Cotswolds. More details for each site can be found within the text for each stage and most sites have high-quality explanatory boards.

The first 'Cotsallers' were nomads, hunter-gatherers who drifted through what was then a heavily wooded region but made little visual impact upon it. It was Neolithic man, around 3000BC, who first began to clear patches in the woodland cover and to till the soil, and in so doing started a primitive form of landscape management. These groups of New Stone Age agriculturalists left behind some 85 burial tombs scattered throughout the region, among the finest being Hetty Pegler's Tump and Belas Knap, both on – or very close to – the Cotswold Way. These ancient relics are typical of what has become known as the Severn–Cotswold Group: large cairns of stone with a covering of soil, and internal passageways lined with drystone walling which open into burial chambers. It has been estimated that some of these tombs must have involved about 15,000 man-hours to build, which indicates a surprising level of social involvement and organisation.

As well as Hetty Pegler's Tump and Belas Knap, there is another similar burial mound of the same period on Frocester Hill (Nympsfield Long Barrow), while at Crickley Hill near Birdlip recent excavations reveal evidence of a 3-acre (1¼-hectare) Neolithic causewayed camp dating from around 3700BC. This contained a village protected by earthwork defences consisting of a double ditch and dry walling topped by a palisade. The discovery of flint arrowheads and items of charred fencing suggest that life in the New Stone Age was not entirely peaceful.

Neolithic man was replaced by tribes of immigrants from the Low Countries. These so-called 'Beaker People' of the Bronze Age lived a mostly nomadic existence, raising stock and undertaking a primitive form of cultivation before moving on. The most significant evidence of their occupation of the Cotswolds is in the form of more than 350 round barrows; however, no major sites from this period are to be seen along the Cotswold Way.

The Iron Age

What is visible on the Cotswold Way, however, is a series of hill and promontory forts dating from the Iron Age, which lasted from about 700BC until the Roman occupation. These are the work of Belgic immigrants known as Dobunni, and it is thought that these defended enclosures served different purposes. Some clearly contained working communities with villages of long houses, while others were market centres or animal corrals, and some of the smaller enclosures were perhaps the fortified homes of Dobunni tribal chieftains. Yet whatever their function, they conformed to set patterns and were protected by deep, rock-cut ditches and tall, near-vertical walls. Nowadays they invariably appear as rounded, grass-covered mounds – some saucer-shaped and distinctive, others with deterioration, perhaps from centuries of ploughing.

There are many fine examples of these hill forts along the route, the largest being at Little Sodbury, where Sodbury Hill Fort covers 11 acres (4½ hectares), enclosed by ditches and earth ramparts. Uley Bury above Dursley is even larger, at more than 30 acres (12 hectares), but is just off the route. Other hill forts may be seen along the way on Cleeve Common, Leckhampton Hill, Crickley Hill and Painswick Beacon, among others.

THE COTSWOLDS SINCE THE ROMANS

The Cotswold Way passes a large number of more recent human developments and monuments from its long and usually prosperous occupation over the past 2000 years. Again, there are many of these, but perhaps the most prominent are:

Stage	Name	Location
1	Wool Market	Chipping Campden
1	Broadway Tower	2km south-east of Broadway
3	Stanway House	Stanway
3	Hailes Abbey	3km north-east of Winchcombe
3/4	Sudeley Castle	1km east of Winchcombe
4	Postlip Hall	Approaching Cleeve Hill, not open to the public
7	Witcombe Roman Villa	Witcombe
10	Tyndale Monument	Above North Nibley
11	Somerset Monument	Near Hawkesbury Upton
12	Horton Court	1km north of Horton village
12	Dodington House	Near Old Sodbury, not open to the public
13	Dyrham Park	Dyrham
14	Royal Crescent and Circus	Bath
14	Roman Baths	Bath
14	Bath Abbey	Bath

The arrival of the Romans

When the Romans came in AD43 they adopted some of the Iron Age camps for their own use. They built fortresses at Corinium (Cirencester) and Glevum (Gloucester), and constructed Ermin Street to link the two; this is crossed by the Cotswold Way at Birdlip. (The similarly named Ermine Street linked London with York).

Away from the towns – and none are greater in this part of Britain than the World Heritage City of Bath – agricultural estates were established and well-to-do citizens built villas for themselves, usually richly decorated with mosaics, on well-chosen sites that caught the sun. The Cotswold Way passes near two of these: one above Wadfield Farm near Winchcombe, the other at Witcombe below Cooper's Hill.

The Saxon era

The Roman occupation of the Cotswolds ended in AD410 with the withdrawal of the legions and the advance of the Saxons. The centuries that followed are shrouded in mystery, but it is thought that these newcomers brought with them a way of life that was not ordered with the same degree of Roman culture and organisation, and there seem to have been many tribal differences to settle. It was during this period that Arthur rose as defender of Britain.

Tales of King Arthur are the stuff of legends, but there is little doubt that these were unsettled times. Towards the end of the sixth century a battle took place on Hinton Hill, near Dyrham, between the West Saxon warlords Cuthwine and Cealwin and three kings of the Britons. The kings – Coinmail, Condidan and Farinmail – were slaughtered and the Britons retreated to Wales and Somerset, leaving the towns of Bath, Cirencester and Gloucester in Saxon hands, where they remained.

The Cotswolds were then ruled by West Saxons in the south, and Mercian Saxons in the north. The Mercian capital was established at Winchcombe where a monastery was founded. At the abbey at Bath, which became an important and substantial Saxon town, King Edgar was crowned the first King of all England in AD973. The Church grew in power, and by the end of the Saxon period it owned a large proportion of the Cotswolds. It was during this period that whole sheepskins were being exported to serve English missionaries and other markets on the continent, an export that began as early as AD700.

Norman rule

Under Norman rule, following the invasion of 1066, the Cotswolds remained a place of some importance in the country, with England's capital being very briefly centred at Gloucester. A new phase of building began, evidence of which can still be seen today, particularly in the churches. Horton Court, a few yards off the route of the Cotswold Way,

Cotswold Lion sheep at Tormarton awaiting its annual shearing (Stage 12)

also dates from Norman times and is still in use.

The Domesday Survey of 1086 showed that the region was already largely cultivated, but with woodland covering much of the western escarpment. More clearings were made during the following centuries and the open fields then turned to extensive sheep pasture. 'In Europe the best wool is English; in England the best wool is Cotswold.' This saying held true throughout the Norman era, when sheep outnumbered people by four to one and exports of Cotswold wool increased accordingly.

The traditional animal of these vast sheepwalks (pastures) was known as the Cotswold Lion, a breed of sheep 'with the whitest wool, having long necks and square bodies'. These long necks were adorned with a shaggy woollen 'mane', which led to their nickname.

By the Middle Ages the wolds were almost entirely given over to grazing these sheep, and the wool masters used their great wealth to build some of the grand houses and elegant 'wool-gothic' churches (complete with lavish stained glass and intricate carvings) that now form such a feature of the Cotswold Way.

Fine examples of such churches passed along the Way include:

Location	Church	Build date
Chipping Campden	St James	14th and 15th century
Broadway	St Michael and All Angels	Victorian
Stanton	St Michael and All Angels	12th and 15th century
Hailes Church	St Nicholas	12th century
Hailes Abbey		13th century
Winchcombe	St Peter	15th century
Painswick	St Mary	11th through to 15th century
Wotton-under-Edge	St Mary the Virgin	13th century
Little Sodbury	St Adeline	Rebuilt 19th century
Old Sodbury	St John the Baptist	13th and 15th century
Tormarton	St Mary Magdalene	12th century
Cold Ashton	Holy Trinity	14th and 16th century
Bath Abbey	St Peter and St Paul	15th century

Chipping Campden owes its architectural splendour to the wool masters; its church is a monument built with the proceeds of wool sales, as are those at Wotton-under-Edge and several other places along the route.

The decline in the export of raw wool began in the early 15th century with crippling taxes. (Revenue from wool at one time accounted for more than half of England's fortune.) But this decline was partly addressed by the home manufacture of cloth, when the new masters of the Cotswolds were mill owners and middlemen who built fine houses for themselves in Painswick and the Stroud Valley, taking over from the sheep owners as financiers of a fresh spate of church-building and creating a new middle class in the process.

The church at Chipping Campden is one of the richest on the route and worth a visit before setting off (Stage 1)

The Civil War and the enclosures

In the 17th century the Civil War was fought here, as elsewhere, forcing a temporary halt in the fortunes that were being made. Along the escarpment several battle sites are passed on the Cotswold Way, among them a hilltop area still known today as the Battlefields, where the Battle of Lansdown, fought on 5 July 1643, saw Royalist attempts to take Bath bloodily rebuffed. The battle was largely a draw, as the Parliamentarians retreated, although they achieved their objective of holding Bath. At the other end of the walk Campden House, next to Chipping Campden's parish church, was taken as a garrison for Royalist troops, but when they left in 1645 they destroyed it by setting it on fire. Painswick's church still bears signs of a Civil War skirmish, and one of the last of the battles was fought on the slopes of Dover's Hill.

Between 1700 and 1840 large areas of open land were enclosed by Acts of Parliament, and this brought about the countryside's greatest change in appearance for hundreds of years. This was when drystone walls and hedges began to divide the wolds into the field patterns we see today. Large estates were planted with shelter belts for the raising of game birds, while the Cotswolds as a whole became much less dependent on sheep and instead became a broader agricultural base with arable land replacing the pastures of old.

To all intents and purposes, this is the landscape explored by walkers of the Cotswold Way in the 21st century.

THE COTSWOLD WAY

Approaching the summit of Cleeve Hill with Cheltenham and the Severn valley in the background

STAGE 1

Chipping Campden to Broadway

Start	Market in Chipping Campden
Finish	Broadway
Distance	9.6km (6 miles)
Ascent	215m
Descent	265m
Time	2hr 45min
Refreshments	Off route at Broadway Tower and Broadway
Accommodation	Broadway

Right from the start, you will be experiencing the very essence of the Cotswolds – high escarpment edges, vast views and the charms of mellow stone villages nestling below. A short climb out of Chipping Campden leads to the first dramatic viewpoint of Dover's Hill, then on through fields and lanes to the vantage point of Broadway Tower, finishing with a descent through meadows to Broadway, an elegant village with its wide avenue of chestnut trees and grand houses.

This first stage combines well with Stage 2 to Stanton for a 4–5hr first day. And if you arrive in Chipping Campden around lunchtime, you can be in Broadway by late afternoon.

CHIPPING CAMPDEN

The elegance of Chipping Campden stems from the wealth generated by the wool trade. In the centre of the village, the 17th-century Market Hall, built in 1627, is a prominent feature with graceful arches. Nearby is the 14th-century Woolstaplers' Hall, which houses the town's museum, opposite which is one of the earliest buildings in the town, Grevel House, dating from 1380.

The Woolstaplers' Hall and the almshouses in Church Street are both monuments to the wealthy London cloth merchant Sir Baptist Hicks who also built Campden House in 1615 (near the Church of St James). The house was burned down in the Civil War, and today just two onion-topped gatehouses and two restored Jacobean banqueting houses remain.

The old market in the centre of Chipping Campden

The nearby Parish Church of St James is a fine example of a 'wool-gothic' church reflecting the wealth bought to the town by the wool trade, as do the fine old buildings of the town, made up of private homes, inns, hotels and restaurants.

Chipping Campden to Dover's Hill (2.1km, 40min)

The official start to the walk is by the Market Hall in Chipping Campden High Street. A large circular plaque denotes the start (or the end for northbound walkers).

Begin by walking south along the High Street and continue ahead along Lower High Street then turn right into Hoo Lane next to St Catherine's Roman Catholic Church. As the road curves right continue on Hoo Lane, which rises ahead, first becoming a farm track then a footpath which

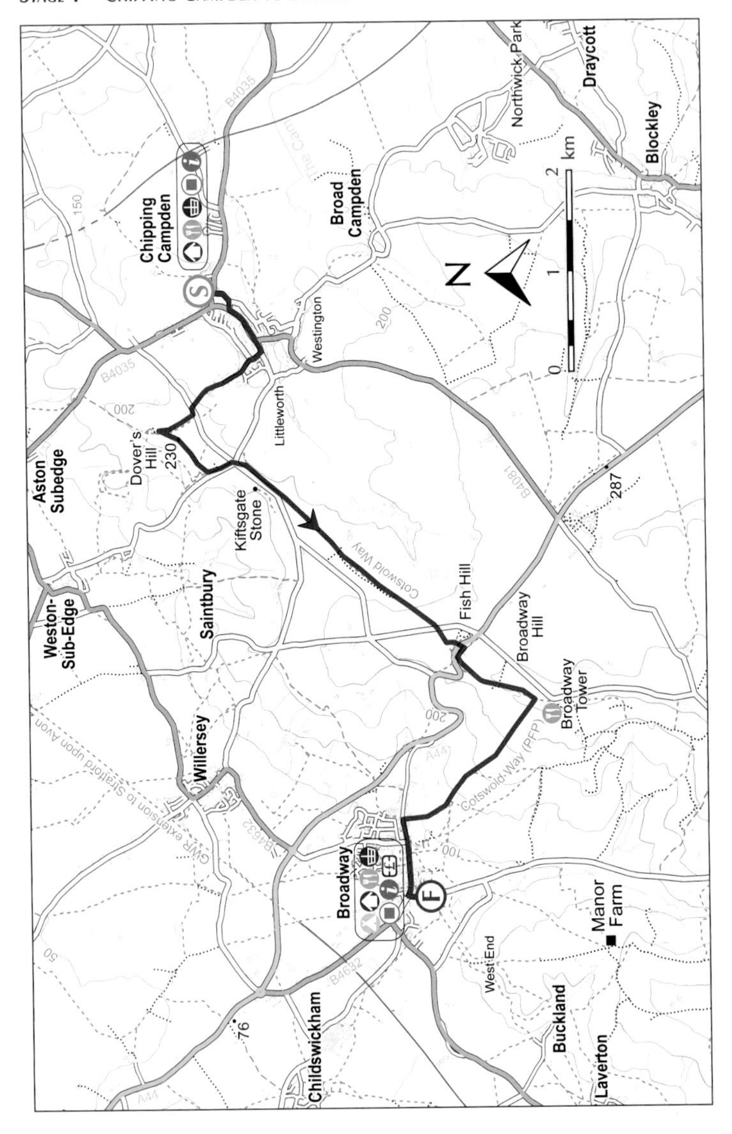

Chipping Campden
Broad Campden
Northwick Park
Draycott
Blockley
Westington
Littleworth
Dover's Hill
230
Aston Subedge
Kiftsgate Stone
Weston-Sub-Edge
Saintbury
Cotswold Way
Fish Hill
Broadway Hill
Broadway Tower
Cotswold Way (PFP)
Willersey
GWR extension to Stratford upon Avon
Broadway
Manor Farm
West End
Buckland
Laverton
Childswickham
B4035
B4081
B4632
A44
287
76
200
150
100
50
N
0
1
2
km

rises to meet Kincombe Lane. Cross the road and turn left, then after 100 metres turn right onto an enclosed path and through a gate to reach **Dover's Hill**, with a trig point just ahead. Turn left and walk across the meadow to a topograph and a memorial stone dedicated to Captain Robert Dover. Dover's Hill is the first edge met on the route and offers fine views to the Malvern Hills.

Acquired by the National Trust in 1926, at 755ft (230m), **Dover's Hill** is one of many fine vantage points along the Cotswold escarpment. It was named after Captain Robert Dover (1582–1652), a wealthy and eccentric lawyer who organised his first 'Olympick Games' there in 1612. The games included leap-frog, wrestling, tug-of-war and 'shin-kicking', and – apart from an interruption during the Civil War – the games continued annually until 1852. Dover's Olympics were revived in 1951 and now take place each spring bank holiday.

Dover's Hill to Fish Hill (3.6km, 1hr)

Pass through a gate into a car park then bear left onto a path running parallel with a narrow lane to reach Kingcomb Lane at a crossroads. Turn right and walk either on the verge or just below along the field margin to reach a stone stile on the left. Maps indicate the location of the Kiftsgate Stone, the possible site of a Saxon meeting place, beside the road and hidden in the trees. It's very hard to find!

Climb over the stone stile then bear right through a gap in a wall which brings you to the Mile Drive, a broad grassy avenue with views to the east. At the end go through a gap in a wall then half-left across a field corner to a second wall. Maintain direction across a field, cross over Buckle Street and continue to reach a picnic area with a topograph on the right just above the A44 at **Fish Hill**. Descend through the picnic area to a car park, then cross the A44 with care just to the right of a toilet block.

Fish Hill to Broadway Tower (1.2km, 20min)

Turn right along a tarmac road which leads onto a track, then a footpath on the edge of woods. Cross a lumpy meadow, the site of an Anglo-Saxon burial ground, then bear half-left into a shallow valley with **Broadway Tower** seen ahead. Access to the tower is through a gate, while the continuing path down to Broadway is to the right of the fence surrounding the tower.

The top of **Broadway Tower** is said to be the highest point in the Cotswolds, at 332m, although Cleeve Common has the highest ground. Occupying a grassy knoll, it commands a panoramic view over the Vale of Evesham. Designed by James Wyatt in 1798 for the sixth Earl of Coventry, the tower is a Norman-style keep with three rounded turrets. The entrance fee is currently £12.

Broadway village spread out below

The tower lies within part of the Broadway Tower Country Park, which includes the 150-year-old Tower Barn (refreshments). A café, information centre and shop are housed in Rookery Barn.

Broadway Tower to Broadway (2.7km, 45min)

At first enclosed by fences, the way descends along the right-hand edge of a grassy slope and through meadows linked by kissing gates to reach **Broadway**. As you come to the village, turn left and walk along the main street heading west. In the heart of the village the street is flanked by red-flowering chestnut trees and lined with buildings of mellow stone, with a broader village green and war memorial.

BROADWAY

A quintessential Cotswold village, with a wide street lined with handsome shops, houses and hotels – hence 'broad way'. It is said to have been 'discovered' by William Morris, in whose wake came a number of Victorian artists to make the village famous. The village has a long history, but during the era of the stagecoach it grew in importance, providing accommodation and a change of horses in readiness for the steep haul up Fish Hill. Nowadays horses have been replaced by horsepower, and Broadway is at times a snarl of traffic amid a clutter of commerce.

Without traffic, the village is a gem: wisteria-clad cottages, 17th-century almshouses, an avenue of chestnut trees, a village green and two churches. The oldest of these is St Eadburgh's, which dates from the 12th century, and the other is the Victorian Church of St Michael and All Angels, passed on the way out of the village.

NORTHBOUND FROM BROADWAY TO CHIPPING CAMPDEN (9.6km, 2hr 50min)

This final short stage begins with a vigorous climb up through meadows to Broadway Tower, the top of which claims to be the highest point in the Cotswolds. There are fine views from here back down to Broadway and extending across the Severn Valley to the Malvern Hills and beyond. An undulating route keeps mostly to the top of the escarpment, dropping slightly to cross the A44 at Fish Hill. Crossing fields then along the Mile Drive, the route reaches Dover's Hill, the final vantage point on the route, before heading down into the historic town of Chipping Campden and the end of the Cotswold Way.

Broadway to Broadway Tower (2.7km, 55min)

From the war memorial on the village green, walk up the main street, then turn right after about 900 metres on a signed track. Go through a gate, across a paddock then bear half-left, where the way now progresses uphill through meadows linked by kissing gates towards **Broadway Tower**. Shortly before you reach the tower the path is enclosed by fences.

Broadway Tower to Fish Hill (1.2km, 20min)

The Cotswold Way breaks to the left across a rough undulating pasture, then down a shallow valley. Pass beside the edge of woodland, and at the end continue on a track which curves to the right onto a tarmac service road leading to the A44 at the top of **Fish Hill**.

Fish Hill to Dover's Hill (3.6km, 1hr)

Cross the road opposite a toilet block at the Fish Hill picnic site. Bear left following waymarks up a grass slope, then turn right at the top just before a topograph. The continuing path takes you across a field to a country road, then over two more fields to join the Mile Drive, and at the far end through a gap in a drystone wall.

Bear right for about 400 metres along the grass verge of the road. On coming to a minor crossroads turn left to a National Trust car park giving access to **Dover's Hill** on the right.

Dover's Hill to Chipping Campden (2.1km, 35min)

Walk ahead to a topograph, then at a trig point bear right to find a kissing gate in the meadow corner leading between fields to Kingcomb Lane. Turn left, then after about 100 metres cross the road onto a descending path leading onto Hoo Lane, then turn left by St Catherine's Roman Catholic Church into **Chipping Campden** High Street. Continue ahead to the Town Hall and the official end of the Cotswold Way.

STAGE 2

Broadway to Stanton

Start	Broadway
Finish	Stanton
Distance	7km (4 miles)
Ascent	235m
Descent	215m
Time	2hr
Refreshments	None until Stanton
Accommodation	Stanton

From Broadway, the continuing route takes you across meadows then back up along the scarp edge on a clear track for a while. On reaching the site of an Iron Age fort at Shenberrow Hill you leave the uplands once more and head steeply down through a cleeve, a dry valley, (which is sometimes quite wet and muddy!) and green meadows to the almost too perfect classic stone village of Stanton.

Broadway to Shenberrow Hill (5.2km, 1hr 30min)

From the village green, turn left into Church Street, passing the Crown and Trumpet, then turn right onto a track opposite the Church of St Michael and All Angels. Follow the path across two meadows to reach a lane, then cross straight over up an enclosed path into a sloping meadow. Pass through a small coppice then continue up to the top of the hill and bear left along the field edge. Pass a barn then maintain direction along a track to reach **Manor Farm**, currently an untidy and muddy farmyard through which you bear right. A rough track keeps to the right of a series of fields then below a line of beeches to gain the crest of a ridge, with Laverton Hill Farm on the left.

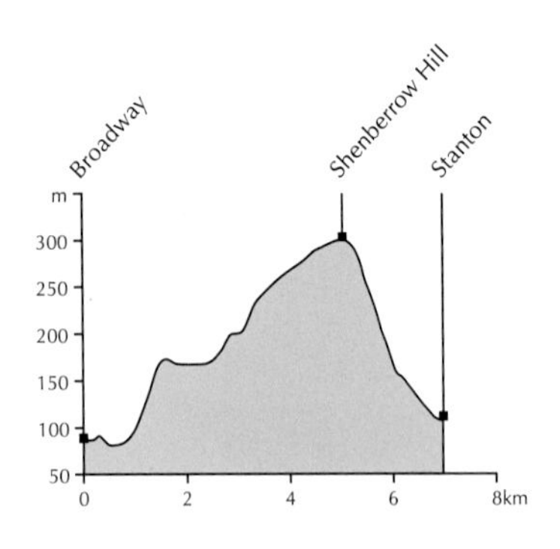

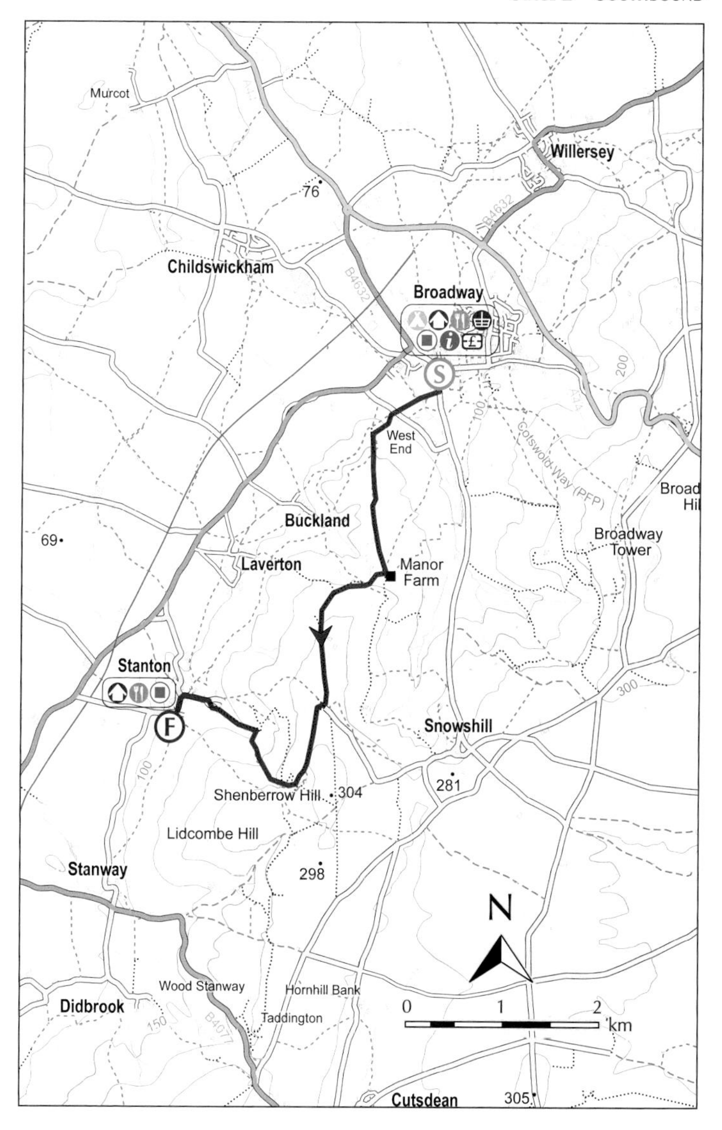
Murcot
Willersey
76
B4632
Childswickham
Broadway
B4632
200
West End
Cotswold Way (PFP)
Broad Hill
Buckland
Broadway Tower
69
Laverton
Manor Farm
Stanton
300
Snowshill
100
281
Shenberrow Hill
304
Lidcombe Hill
298
Stanway
N
Wood Stanway
Hornhill Bank
Didbrook
Taddington
0
1
2
km
150
B4077
Cutsdean
305

The track takes you past a region of old quarries, then 200 metres later join a track for a few metres then turn sharply right over a cattle grid and follow this track as it curves left through more meadows, with Long Hill Plantation on the right to reach **Shenberrow Hill**.

> **Shenberrow Hill** (304m) above Stanton is the site of an Iron Age hill fort of about 2½ acres. When it was excavated in 1935, various artefacts were revealed – among them pieces of pottery, a bronze bracelet and two bone needles.

Shenberrow Hill to Stanton (1.8km, 30min)

At Shenberrow Hill pass to the right of a farm, go through a gate, and immediately descend to the right through a steep-sided cleeve among trees. The path is both steep and often muddy. At the bottom veer left, cross a stile and continue downhill towards a pond in a hollow. Keep the pond to your left, go through a gate then left. A track now leads down to **Stanton**, a small unspoilt village, the main street lined with classic Cotswold stone houses; at the far end of the street is a stone cross which uniquely incorporates a sundial, and the village church.

Thatched cottage passed entering Stanton

STANTON

It has been called the perfect Cotswold village, and not without good reason. There was a farming settlement in the area as early as 2500BC, and a village developed on the spring line as early as the 9th century. The village is made up of a group of 16th-century cottages and farmhouses (Stanton, or Stan Tun, meaning 'stony farm') built from local stone, uniformly lining the main street towards the church, and beyond.

When Sir Philip Stott came to Stanton Court in 1906, he found the village rather neglected, and for the next 30 years until his death he invested in the restoration of the village to the splendour we see today. Unlike Broadway, Stanton is not on a main thoroughfare, and remains a quiet backwater except for walkers, horse riders and tourists who come to photograph the scenery.

NORTHBOUND FROM STANTON TO BROADWAY (7km, 2hr)

The Cotswold Way leaves Stanton to climb steeply across fields and up through a narrow cleeve to reach the Iron Age hill fort at Shenberrow Hill. From there, the way follows the scarp edge before descending steadily on a track, then on paths across fields to reach Broadway.

Stanton to Shenberrow Hill (1.8km, 40min)

From the stone cross and sundial walk up through the picture-perfect village of Stanton and bear right just before the end of the main street, then bend left to follow a rising track, often muddy near the bottom. Follow a waymark to the right through a gate, then keep to the right of a sloping field, go through another field, then go up into a narrow cleeve, which is often wet and slippery, to reach the site of an Iron Age hill fort at **Shenberrow Hill.**

Shenberrow Hill to Broadway (5.2km, 1hr 20min)

Turn left and follow the track ahead, and at a cattle grid turn left then right to continue, now heading slightly downhill to reach an untidy and muddy cluster of farm buildings (**Manor Farm**) on the edge of Buckland Wood. Bear left on a continuation of the track for nearly 800 metres then over a stile on the right. Pass a barn on your left and enter Broadway Coppice. Descend through the little wood and continue down the slope to an enclosed path which leads to West End Lane.

Cross the lane and continue directly ahead through linking fields and over a footbridge, then on a track leading into Church Street, almost opposite the Parish Church of St Michael and All Angels in Broadway. Turn left down the street to the green, then go right to reach the war memorial on the village green in **Broadway**.

St Michael and All Angels church in Broadway

STAGE 3

Stanton to Winchcombe

Start	Stanton
Finish	Winchcombe
Distance	12.3km (7¾ miles)
Ascent	270m
Descent	280m
Time	3hr 15min
Refreshments	Hayles Fruit Farm and Winchcombe
Accommodation	Stanway, Wood Stanway, North Farmcote, Hayles Fruit Farm, Winchcombe

Between Stanton and Wood Stanway, the route stays low with no climbs. Crossing manicured parkland, the route passes the vast mansion of Stanway House and its obedient village and rebuilt water mill before a final level section heads through a thoroughly park-like setting into the hamlet of Wood Stanway, with B&B accommodation.

A stiff climb out of Wood Stanway reveals the edges and broad views into the vale below, with a curious line of single trees marking boundaries on the windy plateau. At Stumps Cross the route avoids the road and takes a good track before passing Beckbury Hill Fort and a monument, reputed to be the place from which Thomas Cromwell watched the destruction of the substantial Hailes Abbey below. A steep descent reaches the Hayles Fruit Farm, with Hailes Abbey just below.

Allow time to explore Hailes Abbey and museum, managed by English Heritage. Just opposite is the tiny ancient Hailes Church, which predates the abbey.

Stanton to Wood Stanway (3.6km, 1hr)

From the cross in Stanton, head onwards to the junction and turn left. At the end of the street continue ahead on a path between houses and out across open fields, interspersed with small copses. Cross several fields and drop slightly into **Stanway**. Turn left along the road past Stanway House, the church and the impressive gatehouse.

The elegant gatehouse of Stanway House

Stanway is even smaller than Stanton – a clutch of buildings arranged around the Jacobean manor, Stanway House. In almost 1300 years of ownership, the manor has changed hands only once (except by inheritance), and the village seems unchanged for centuries.

As well as the manor and 12th-century Church of St Peter, there is a massive tithe barn in the grounds of the manor. The grand entrance to Stanway House is through an impressive three-storey Jacobean gatehouse, with gables decorated with giant scallop-shells. Also in the village is a restored 13th-century watermill (operating and producing stone-ground flour, available to buy during high summer) which once belonged to the abbots of Tewkesbury – this is open only in the summer months.

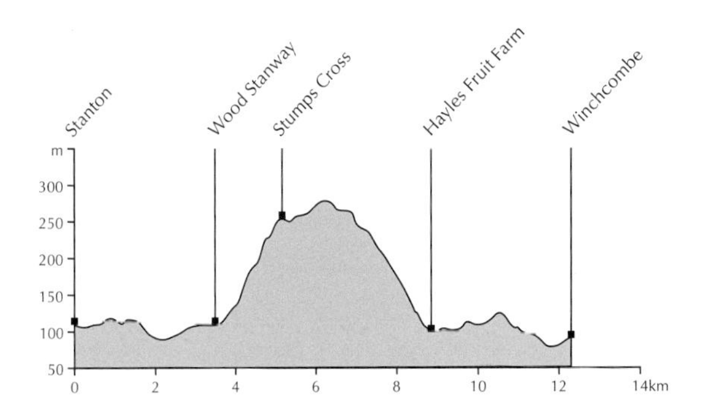

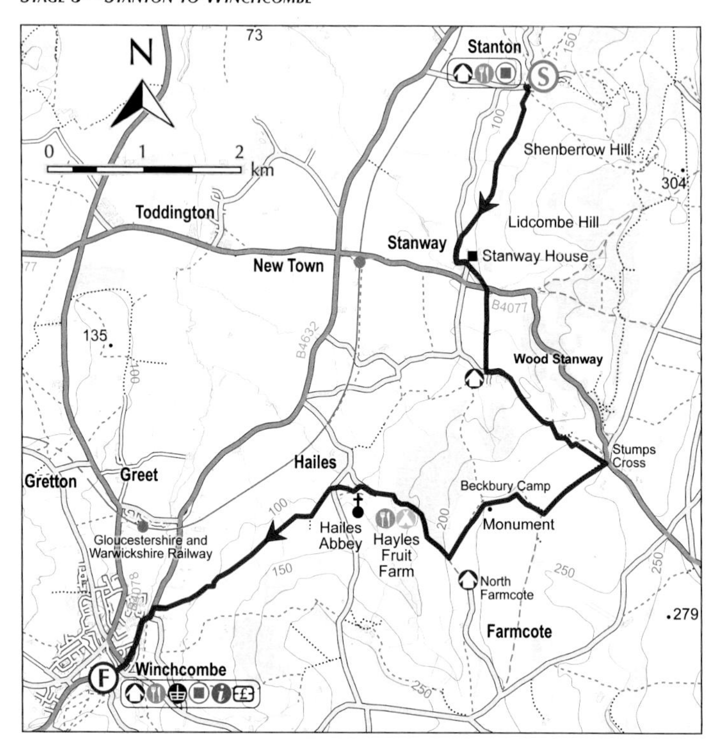

Bear left alongside a stream and past the water mill. Cross the B4077 road and walk by a fence alongside fields on a path into **Wood Stanway**.

Wood Stanway to Hayles Fruit Farm (4.9km, 1hr 15min)

Turn left entering Wood Stanway (turn right for B&B accommodation at Wood Stanway Farm), passing substantial houses to the left and right, and pass through the yards at Glebe Farm, which may be muddy. Climb the fields on a path which is sometimes just a slight colouring of the grassy slopes, passing Lower Coscombe Farm. A final steep section rises diagonally to a wall; leave this to the right and come to the B4077 road at **Stumps Cross**.

Turn right along a good track and after 15min, follow the CW right where it descends a field to pass **Beckbury Camp** and the remote **monument**.

Beckbury Camp is the site of an Iron Age hill fort extending to over 4 acres. It originally consisted of a single ditch and rampart. The ditch has since been filled; however, along the east side the position of the rampart is still visible. As with so many of the hill forts in the Cotswolds, its position on the scarp edge would have made it comparatively easy to defend.

Follow the path very steeply through a small copse and across open fields to meet a lane. Turn right down the stony track and, where it meets the road, find the entrance to Hayles Fruit Farm. Hailes Abbey is 250 metres further down the road.

Accommodation can be found at **North Farmcote**. Camping and an excellent café can be found at **Hayles Fruit Farm**.

HAILES ABBEY

It is still possible to imagine the monastic life at Hailes Abbey among the ruins

Managed and maintained by English Heritage, Hailes Abbey was built in 1246 by Richard Earl of Cornwall, brother of Henry III, as a thanksgiving for having survived a near-shipwreck. The abbey was home to a community of Cistercian monks and, when a phial purporting to contain the blood of Christ was presented by Richard's second son Edmund in 1270, Hailes became a place of pilgrimage for nearly 300 years. In 1538 the phial was taken to London for analysis, where the contents were pronounced as nothing more than 'honey clarified and coloured with saffron'. The abbey was destroyed in 1539 during the country-wide dissolution of the monasteries under Henry VIII. Its splendour is mostly lost, although the ruins are still evocative of the past. A museum displays several artefacts from the site. Just opposite is the tiny ancient Hailes Church of St Nicholas. Built in 1175, its walls are decorated with beautiful 12th-century paintings.

Hailes Abbey and its museum are open from April to October, 10:00–16:00 (closed on Monday and Tuesday) – weekends from November to March.

Hayles Fruit Farm to Winchcombe (3.8km, 1hr)
Continue downhill from the turn to Hayles Farm and pass the substantial remains of **Hailes Abbey**. Opposite the village church turn left across a meadow, join a road by a line of houses and turn right, then in 100 metres turn left onto ancient Salters Lane. In 5min a path heads right and across fields, some of which have crops, so may be muddy. Dip down to cross a stream on a bridge and press on. The path merges into a lane (Puck Pit Lane). Follow this to a road (the B4632) and turn left to follow the road into the centre of **Winchcombe**.

WINCHCOMBE

Winchcombe is only a small town, but with a local vibrancy that sets it apart from the other towns and villages visited so far. The main street is flanked by a pleasing mixture of Cotswold stone buildings. Once an important settlement, Winchcombe was the capital of a Saxon shire and seat of Mercian royalty. Offa, King of Mercia, dedicated a nunnery here in AD790, and an abbey was established by his successor, Kenulf, in AD811. Kenulf had a son, Kenelm, who was murdered at the behest of his ambitious sister, and following Kenelm's death assorted miracles were attributed to him which, in turn, made Winchcombe a place of pilgrimage.

The abbey has gone, but the 15th-century parish church of St Peter was partly paid for by abbey funds. Among its more notable features are the 40 gargoyles. The town also displays a pair of wooden stocks, located outside the Folk Museum, and among its buildings are two or three fine old inns, and Tudor houses and cottages. Just 1km east of Winchcombe stands Sudeley Castle, details of which are given in the route description for Stage 4. Vineyard Street, which leads the route out of town, was formerly known as Duck Street, where there was once a ducking stool in the river Isbourne.

The tourist information centre and museum are open daily from April to October, 10:00–16:00, and at weekends between November and March.

NORTHBOUND FROM WINCHCOMBE TO STANTON (12.3km, 3hr 20min)

Initially the route stays low across undulating fields to reach the ruined abbey at Hailes. The ruins are managed by English Heritage and are worth a visit, as is the tiny church opposite. A little further on, there is a camping field in the grounds of Hayles Fruit Farm, which also has a good café. Now the trail rises on a stony track then climbs across meadows to a monument and hill fort at Beckbury on the scarp edge. After a couple of kilometres over high meadows the trail plunges across fields to the hamlet of Wood Stanway, then continues on level ground over more fields to Stanway, with its impressive manor house and almost feudal cluster of cottages and houses. The final section of trail to Stanton crosses undulating parkland and a succession of fields to reach the quiet village of Stanton.

Winchcombe to Hayles Fruit Farm (3.8km, 1hr)

From the museum and tourist information centre, walk through the town and, after crossing the river, turn right into Puck Pit Lane. Cross a stile and walk through a series of undulating fields to reach a track. Bear left and at Salter's Lane turn right then left after 100 metres onto a track past some houses, then go across a field – the ruins of **Hailes Abbey** can be seen on the right. Turn right and walk up the road past Hailes Church and the abbey ruins to the end of the road. **Hayles Fruit Farm** (café and campsite) is up the driveway to the right.

View approaching Winchcombe from the south

Old houses in Winchcombe

Hayles Fruit Farm to Wood Stanway (4.9km, 1hr 25min)

The route continues ahead (left) on a rising track in woods. Then, soon after the wood ends, turn left. (For B&B accommodation at **North Farmcote**, continue up the track for a further 300 metres.) Climb diagonally across meadows heading towards a clump of trees, where there is a small memorial at **Beckbury Camp Hill Fort**.

Turn left following the field boundary all the way then pass through a gap in the wall and resume direction towards a little woodland to meet a crossing track. Bear left along the track (known as Campden Lane) for about 800 metres, leading to the B4077 at **Stumps Cross**.

Turn sharply left round a wall and through a gate heading north-east to the lip of the escarpment. Descend the slope to the left of a house, then cross several meadows signed with marker posts to Glebe Farm and onto a metalled road in the hamlet of **Wood Stanway**.

Wood Stanway to Stanton (3.6km, 55min)

Turn right before Wood Stanway House (B&B available) and walk along the left-hand boundaries of successive low-lying fields to the B4077 on the outskirts of Stanway. Go left for about 40 metres, turn right to cross a small meadow, then continue on a footpath past a restored watermill and into the hamlet of **Stanway**.

Soon after passing Stanway House, take a stile on the right opposite the cricket ground into parkland. Waymark posts guide the route. Follow the continuing footpath over several fields skirting the foot of the slope. Enter the village and bear left on a farm drive. This leads to a road where you turn right into the village of **Stanton**.

STAGE 4

Winchcombe to Cleeve Hill

Start	Winchcombe
Finish	Cleeve Hill Golf Course Clubhouse
Distance	9.2km (5¾ miles)
Ascent	360m
Descent	200m
Time	3hr
Refreshments	None until Cleeve Hill
Accommodation	Postlip Farm, Cleeve Hill

Leave Winchcombe near its beautiful church, descend a street lined with ancient cottages decorated with flowers and enter lush meadows below Sudeley Castle before climbing past sports fields and then across a steadily rising pasture. Skirt fields and pass through ancient beech woods to reach one of the route's absolute highlights, the long barrow of Belas Knap.

Having considered the lives of our long-dead ancestors, leave Belas Knap and descend into Breakheart Plantation – a steep descent in a fine old mixed woodland suffering from ash dieback. Keep dropping down to cross a stream and then climb past a farm before dropping again to the impressive Postlip Hall and its tithe barn.

Pass around the Hall and enter the open access land of Cleeve Common on a good track into the golf course. Signs suggest being aware of adders, so keep dogs under close control. Views of Cheltenham far below and the entire Severn valley open up, one of the most impressive sights of the route.

Winchcombe to Belas Knap (3.5km, 1hr 20min)

From Winchcombe Tourist Information Centre by the central road junction, continue along the main street, first passing a steeply descending road, then turn left on Vineyard Street. Descend the road between houses and cross the river Isbourne on an old bridge. Turn immediately right across meadows on a well-made path to reach Corndean Lane. Turn left and, after 400 metres, branch right on a track and pass a sports ground, then a riding school.

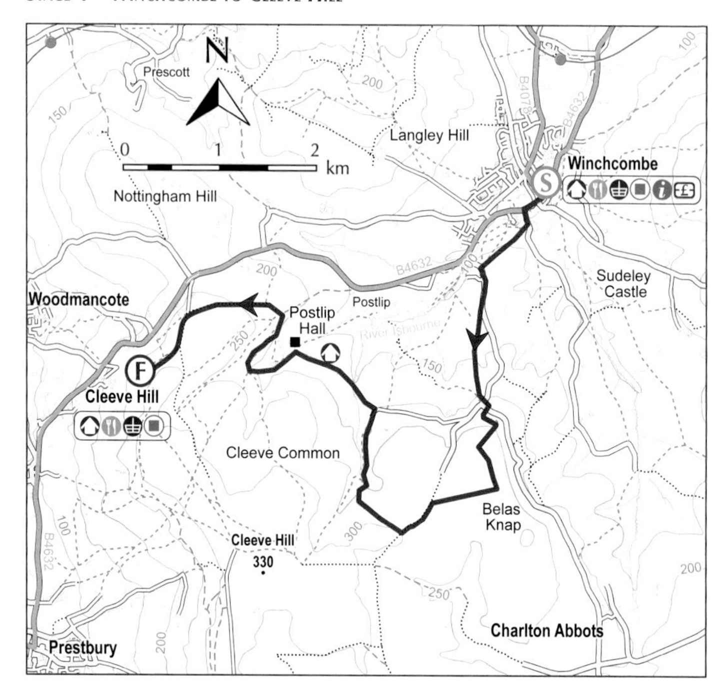

Turn left opposite the riding school and climb a large field to meet Corndean Lane again. Take the path ahead above the road, then right to climb into woods and emerge in a field. A path heads straight across, but the official CW keeps left along the bottom of the field before climbing. You are guided to a path by the field side – follow this to **Belas Knap**.

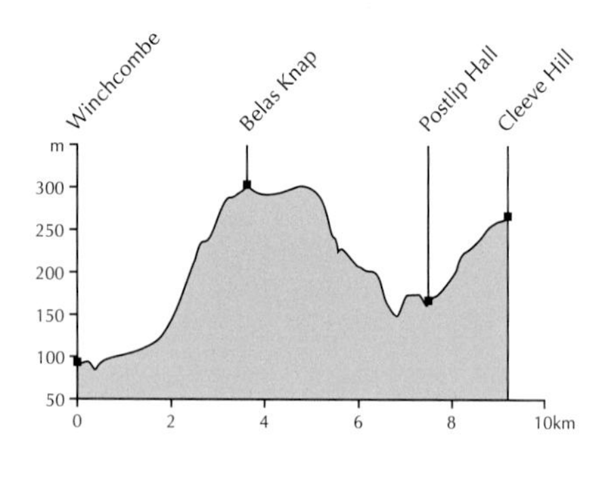

SUDELEY CASTLE

The present Sudeley Castle dates from the 15th century – it is a rebuilding by Ralph Boteler of an earlier 12th-century castle. Boteler, who became lord chancellor and was made Baron Sudeley, created a magnificent building, but he backed the wrong side in the Wars of the Roses and his property was confiscated by Edward IV.

The castle eventually passed into the hands of Henry VIII, after whose death his widow, Katherine Parr, married Lord Seymour and came to live here. Shortly after giving birth to a daughter, Mary, in 1548, Katherine died. She is buried in a lead coffin in St Mary's Chapel.

The castle is still occupied, and several rooms – including the remains of the Elizabethan banqueting hall, the tithe barn, Portmore Tower and St Mary's Chapel – all survive and are open to the public, as are the extensive grounds.

Open daily between April and October, 10:00–16:00, www.sudeleycastle.co.uk.

BELAS KNAP

Belas Knap is a striking example of a chambered tomb, or long barrow, of which there are many in the Severn–Cotswold region. The name means hilltop beacon, which suggests that the site was used by the Saxons who occupied Winchcombe at the foot of the escarpment. Belas Knap dates from about 3600BC. It's a large wedge-shaped mound measuring some 178ft (54 metres) long, 60ft (18 metres) wide and about 13ft (4 metres) at its highest point. At its northern end is a false portal with two horns lined with drystone walling and blocked by a massive slab.

Looking at the interior of Belas Knap

When it was excavated in 1863, the remains of five children and the skull of an adult were discovered behind the portal.

Approaching Postlip Hall

There are two chambers along the eastern side, one on the west and another at the southern end, reached by shallow passages walled with stones laid in almost identical fashion to many of the drystone walls seen along the Cotswold Way. No less than 26 burials took place in the paired north-east and north-west chambers, and the remains of two males and two females were found in the south-eastern chamber. The 1863 excavation also revealed Roman coins and pottery.

Belas Knap to Postlip Hall (3.9km, 1hr 10min)
Follow the route along a field wall, keeping to this as the path bears left. Turn right after 400 metres, again alongside a field, and descend into Breakheart Plantation. Descend steeply before rising and falling again. Pass a house (Woodpeckers) and turn left where a road joins from the right. Drop down the field and into woods again before crossing the stream and climbing a field side. The farm ahead has a number of feed lots and can be incredibly muddy, but can be bypassed by a permissive route through a field above. Rejoin the track and pass Postlip Farm (B&B) before descending in full view of **Postlip Hall**.

Postlip Hall to Cleeve Hill (1.8km, 30min)

Take a path to the left by a wall just before Postlip Hall and follow past stables and farm buildings as the wall turns right. Keep alongside the wall (passing the gushing spring to the left) and through gates onto Cleeve Common. Follow the track along the common's edge, climbing gently, to enter the golf course, and soon reach the welcoming clubhouse.

POSTLIP HALL

The original medieval hall dates from the 15th century, although it has been extended over many years and the main Jacobean frontage was added in 1614. A large tithe barn in the grounds dates from sometime between 1140 and 1400, while the chapel is 12th century. The house is now divided into eight separate units, and the occupants collectively share the maintenance of the house and grounds.

Accommodation is available at Postlip Farm B&B and refreshments can be found at the Cleeve Hill Golf Club. Other hotel and B&B accommodation is 500 metres ahead in the village of **Cleeve Hill** below.

CLEEVE COMMON

At the heart of the Cotswolds Area of Outstanding Natural Beauty, Cleeve Common includes the highest point on the Cotswolds escarpment, at 330m. Most of this area consists of agriculturally unimproved limestone grassland, which is rarely found elsewhere. It covers an area of over 400 hectares (1000 acres) and is designated a Grade 1 Site of Special Scientific Interest for its geology, habitats and botany, and it contains three Scheduled Monuments. Various orchids, glow-worms, and many different types of butterflies are attracted and protected by the range of habitats found here.

The Common is popular with walkers and golfers; however, there are large areas that still feel wild and remote. Because of its height, this large upland plateau can be swept by mists; when this happens it can be a bleak and mysterious place, and route-finding can be more challenging. But in good conditions vast panoramic views are revealed across the Severn plains towards the Malvern Hills and Bannau Brycheiniog (the Brecon Beacons).

Looking down from Cleeve Hill towards the Malvern Hills over Bishops Cleeve and the Severn Valley

NORTHBOUND FROM CLEEVE HILL TO WINCHCOMBE (9.2km, 2hr 40min)

This stage is full of interest as it leaves and reascends the escarpment on the way to Winchcombe. Descending from Cleeve Hill on a good track, the path traces the walls past Postlip Hall, but it's not until you climb the tarmac road away from Postlip Hall that you can turn and admire its true scale and setting, against the backdrop of Cleeve Hill. Beyond Postlip Farm lies Breakheart Plantation, a beautiful area through which the trail climbs again to regain the escarpment. The route continues along a track and over fields to reach the impressive restored long barrow of Belas Knap. After absorbing the information and peering into the chambers, continue along a path then across a series of fields descending all the time to eventually arrive at the bustling market town of Winchcombe.

Cleeve Hill to Postlip Hall (1.8km, 30min)
With the clubhouse on your left, take the sandy track descending gently, pass through two gates then descend, bearing right to follow beside the boundary wall of **Postlip Hall**. Turn left through a stable yard and continue beside the wall to reach a small road. Turn right and walk up the road past Postlip Hall Farm (B&B available).

Postlip Hall to Belas Knap (3.9km, 1hr 10min)
Continue through (or avoid in a field to the right on a permissive path) the often muddy farmyard, then take the path on the left beside a field, cross a stream and climb up through Breakheart Wood. Emerging from the woods keep to the right side of a field then turn left onto a track. After 400 metres, go right through a gateway and keep to the left margin of a large field to arrive at the restored long barrow of **Belas Knap**.

Belas Knap to Winchcombe (3.5km, 1hr)
The path now heads left (north) beside woods, then continues on the right side of a large sloping field. A gate at the bottom left of the field leads into woods down a steep track. After this, turn left onto a path just above a lane. Continue in the same direction at a junction of lanes through a gate then down a sloping meadow to reach Corndean Lane. Turn left, then after about 400 metres turn right into more fields, maintaining this direction to meet a road on the outskirts of Winchcombe. Turn left, cross the river and walk up Vineyard Street. At the top, turn right and walk into the centre of **Winchcombe** to the crossroads by the museum and tourist information centre.

STAGE 5

Cleeve Hill to Dowdeswell

Start	Cleeve Hill Golf Course Clubhouse
Finish	A40 crossing at Dowdeswell
Distance	9km (5½ miles)
Ascent	180m
Descent	330m
Time	2hr 30min
Refreshments	None until Dowdeswell
Accommodation	Camping above Dowdeswell, otherwise none until Dowdeswell

A peak, a fort and a butterfly reserve – this short stage covers much of the best of the CW. At 317m, the summit reached on Cleeve Common rewards with fine views. Much of the route is on ancient 'unimproved' limestone grassland, with a short road section before crossing fields and continuing through woods down to the A40 on the outskirts of Cheltenham. This short stage provides ample time to explore Cheltenham later in the day, or to be combined with Stage 4 or 6 for a longer stage. Buses to Cheltenham run regularly, and there are good refreshments and shops (and cider) at Dunkertons Organic Cider Centre.

Cleeve Hill to road near Piccadilly Farm (5.2km, 1hr 30min)

From the Cleeve Hill Golf Clubhouse, head right, climbing gradually on the lower of two paths (the higher path is the rambling Winchcombe Way). Pass old quarry sites, now appearing as vast bunkers to entrap unwary golfers, and bear left through gorse bushes onto a steeply climbing path that heads to a vantage point with a trig point. This 317m summit is the highest point on the CW, with excellent views over Cheltenham and the River Severn basin, although the highest point of Cleeve Common at 330m is some way off the route.

Head directly down (south) from the summit, striding out over the cropped grass. Pass a golf green and more quarried ground before reaching the top of a steep edge with a bird's eye view of the farms below. Follow this to the **Cleeve Hill Camp Hill Fort** (sometimes known as Cleeve Cloud Camp), one of the clearest ancient earthworks etched into the CW route.

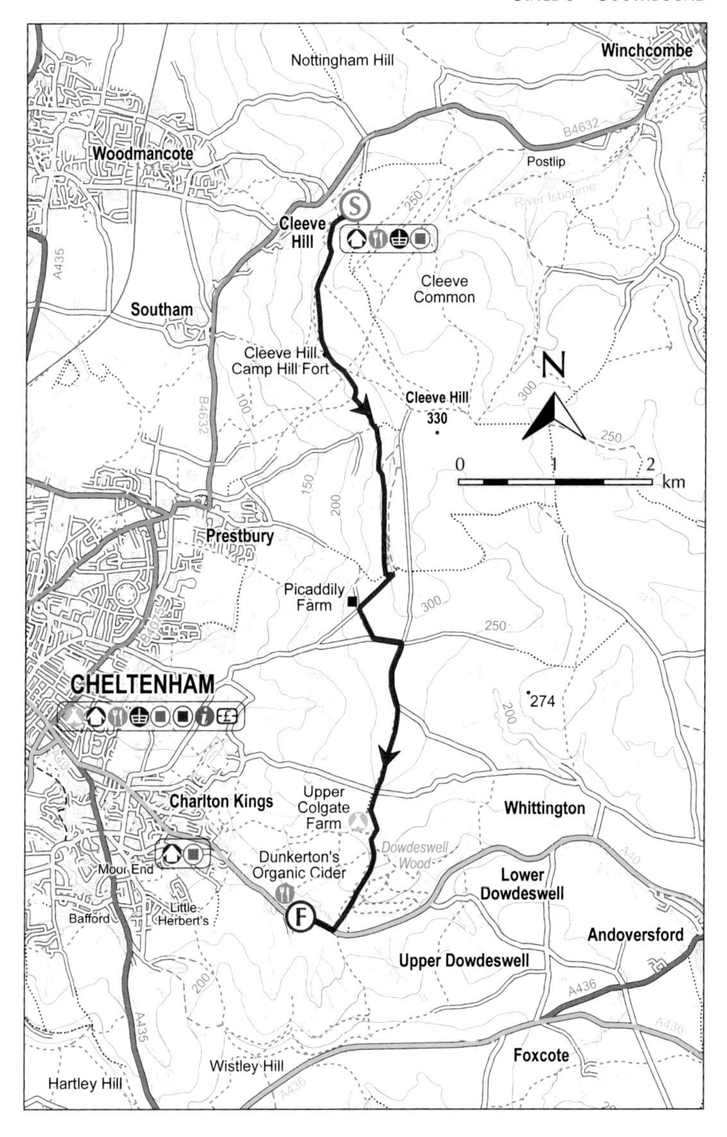
Nottingham Hill
Winchcombe
B4632
Woodmancote
Postlip
River Isbourne
Cleeve Hill
Cleeve Common
A435
Southam
Cleeve Hill Camp Hill Fort
Cleeve Hill
330
N
0
1
2
km
B4632
Prestbury
Picaddily Farm
CHELTENHAM
274
A40
Charlton Kings
Upper Colgate Farm
Whittington
Dowdeswell Wood
Moor End
Dunkerton's Organic Cider
Lower Dowdeswell
Bafford
Little Herbert's
Andoversford
Upper Dowdeswell
A436
A435
Foxcote
Wistley Hill
Hartley Hill

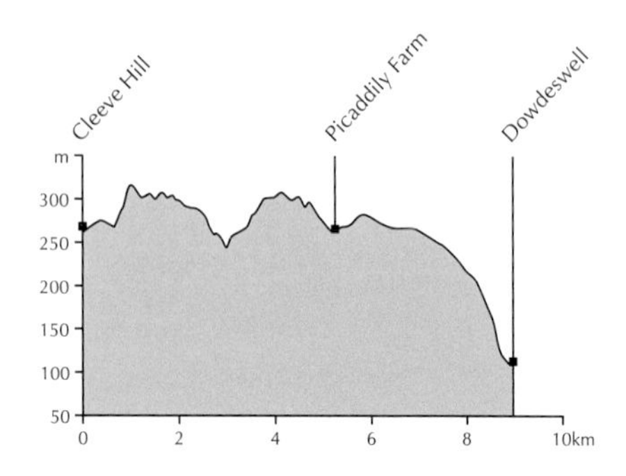

Continue along the edge, gradually descending among gorse bushes, which are bright yellow in springtime. Pass the edge of the Masts Field Butterfly Reserve and turn left on a short steep climb before entering the Bill Smyllie Nature Reserve. Together these make up the Prestbury Hill Butterfly Reserve. Head into a shallow fold in the hillside known as Happy Valley before crossing open ground with low scrub around. Keep left then immediately right and descend a stony track to reach the road near **Piccadilly Farm**.

The rare butterfly haven of Happy Valley

PRESTBURY HILL BUTTERFLY RESERVE

This nature reserve lies on the southern fringes of Cleeve Common and comprises two areas, the Masts Field reserve and the larger Bill Smyllie Reserve to the south. Most of the area is unimproved limestone grassland with abundant herb-rich vegetation and wildlife. As well as a home for butterflies, the area has a wide variety of birds such as skylarks, cuckoos, yellowhammers, stonechats, kestrels, buzzards and a slowly growing population of red kites. Glow-worms, grasshoppers, rabbits, badgers, stoats, weasels and roe deer are also common. Be aware, adders are often seen in spring and summer, as are slow worms, grass snakes and common lizards.

Road near Piccadilly Farm to Dowdeswell (3.8km, 1hr)

At the road, turn left along a field and left at the next small road, then right at the next junction after 400 metres. Follow the road and after 10min keep straight on a path enclosed by hedges on both sides. Cross another road, keep ahead and pass **Upper Colgate Farm** (camping) before being guided into the descent of Dowdeswell Wood, a fine nature reserve with a carpet of flowers in spring. At the bottom, follow the reservoir access track which swings right to meet the A40.

Dowdeswell Reservoir was created in the late 19th century by damming the river Chelt upstream of Charlton Kings, in order to supply the needs of the fast-growing town of Cheltenham. Despite its proximity to the Cotswold Way, it can barely be seen.

If heading directly to Birdlip, climb to the road and cross carefully. Keep right if in need of refreshments or headed to accommodation in Charlton Kings or Cheltenham (40min walk, or 10min by bus). One of the great surprises of the CW is 5min down the A40 – **Dunkertons** organic cider and street food market (including bakery and shop) – so the 5min walk is highly recommended. An early breakfast can be found here for those who overnight in Charlton Kings.

Camping is available at Upper Colgate Farm. Shop and refreshments can be found at **Dowdeswell**. Hotel and shops can be found in Charlton Kings. All facilities are available in Cheltenham.

Cleeve Hill Golf Club and café

NORTHBOUND FROM DOWDESWELL TO CLEEVE HILL (9km, 2hr 40min)

Although this is only a short stage, the route climbs just over 200m, fairly steeply at first on a good path through the beautiful Dowdeswell Wood and Reservoir Nature Reserve, then on paths and tracks across gently rising farmland to briefly join two small country roads. Leaving on a stony track, further height is gained as the path weaves through the Bill Smyllie and Masts Hill nature reserves before finally emerging among gorse bushes up onto Cleeve Common. An impressive set of ramparts are crossed and the scarp edge is followed until the path across cropped grass heads directly to a trig point and topograph, from which there are stunning long-distance views over Cheltenham to the Malvern Hills and mountains of Wales. A steep grassy descent then easy track lead directly to the golf clubhouse, with its excellent café.

Dowdeswell to road near Piccadilly Farm (3.8km, 1hr 10min)
From the A40 descend to the reservoir access track, following it round, then climb through the Dowdeswell Wood and Reservoir Nature Reserve. At the top of the woods cross straight over the farm road and continue ahead. Camping is available at **Upper Colgate Farm** to the left.

Continue across fields, cross a lane, then continue on an enclosed bridleway to join another small lane going in the same direction. At a crossroads turn left, then after about 400 metres turn right onto a track.

Road near Piccadilly Farm to Cleeve Hill (5.2km, 1hr 30min)
At the next junction turn up to the right and climb to the scarp edge. Watch for a sharp turn left then immediately right by a small abandoned quarry. The path leads into a shallow valley known as Happy Valley, part of the Bill Smyllie Nature Reserve. Follow the clear path through the reserve, then at the end of a small wood turn down to the left then immediately right along the lower edge of the Masts Field Butterfly Reserve. The path now curves and climbs between hawthorn and gorse bushes to reach a gate onto Cleeve Common.

Keeping near the edge of the escarpment, pass through the **Cleeve Hill Camp** Iron Age fort, then continue with Castle Rock protruding ahead, following waymarks away from the edge towards a trig point and topograph at 317m. Head slightly left and descend steeply at first to join a good clear track which leads across the hillside to the **Cleeve Hill Golf Clubhouse** (refreshments).

Accommodation, if needed, is in the village below the golf course.

STAGE 6

Dowdeswell to Birdlip

Start	A40 crossing at Dowdeswell
Finish	Road 5min below Birdlip
Distance	16.7km (10½ miles)
Ascent	495m
Descent	350m
Time	4hr 30min
Refreshments	Seven Springs, National Star College, Crickley Hill Visitor Centre, Birdlip
Accommodation	Birdlip, camping at Seven Springs

This stage goes through a mixture of woodlands, fields and elevated grassy hilltops with the most spectacular views. Attractive Lineover Wood can be muddy when wet. A transitional section passes the National Star Training College for disabled students (refreshments) and a series of long barrows before continuing into the beautiful Crickley Hill Country Park – a nature reserve full of flowers, birdlife and woodland – to reach the fine viewpoint and important archaeological site of Crickley Hill, occupied for over 6000 years.

Crickley Hill hill fort archaeological site and visitor centre is located within Crickley Hill Country Park, and it's worth taking some time here if possible, as it is one of the leading archaeological sites in England. Although there is no accommodation on or near the route, there are two or three opportunities for refreshments along the way.

To reach Birdlip, the steady descent from Crickley Hill meets the A416/A417 junction. Road works in the area are likely to affect the precise routing throughout the life of this edition. Climbing again on the edge, views are now over Gloucester and beyond before a finale through woods to reach Birdlip.

This stage can be combined with Stage 5 from Cleeve Common, making for a long day.

Dowdeswell to Seven Springs (4.6km, 1hr 20min)

Cross the A40 – a very busy road – to the east of the Indian restaurant, cross a field and climb into Lineover Wood. The track is good and climbs nearly 200m within a single km. Higher up, the path heads up through fields before turning right and into woods again. Staying below the A436 road, return to woodland, walking on a path that can be muddy in the wet. This stays high before dropping down **Wistley Hill** to meet the road. A path in fields heads to the **Seven Springs** round junction and its eponymous pub.

Camping (and glamping) at Big Skies Glamping above Wistley Grove.

It is thought that **Seven Springs** may be the true source of the river Thames, since it is the source of the River Churn, a tributary of the Thames. The springs leak from the water table beneath Hartley Hill. Since they never run dry – unlike the springs at Lechlade, the other possible source of the Thames – many consider Seven Springs to be a more plausible candidate.

Seven Springs to Leckhampton Hill (3.0km, 50min)

Find the small road heading just to the west of the A435 from Seven Springs (the second road on the right as you approach). This climbs gradually towards Charlton Kings Common. Where the road turns sharply left, continue straight ahead on a track, turning left again after 200 metres. Follow the path round the field and then onto the common, rising gently with benches where you can stop to admire the extensive views from the top. Views include the Malvern Hills Black Mountains and the Brecon Beacons in Wales. Weave in and out of woods and gorse bushes to reach the trig point summit of **Leckhampton Hill** (293m); the best viewpoint is 200 metres further on, right on the scarp edge. The Devil's Chimney is below to the left.

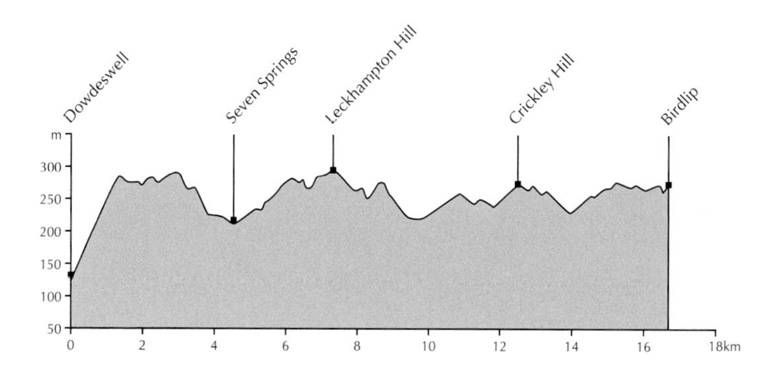

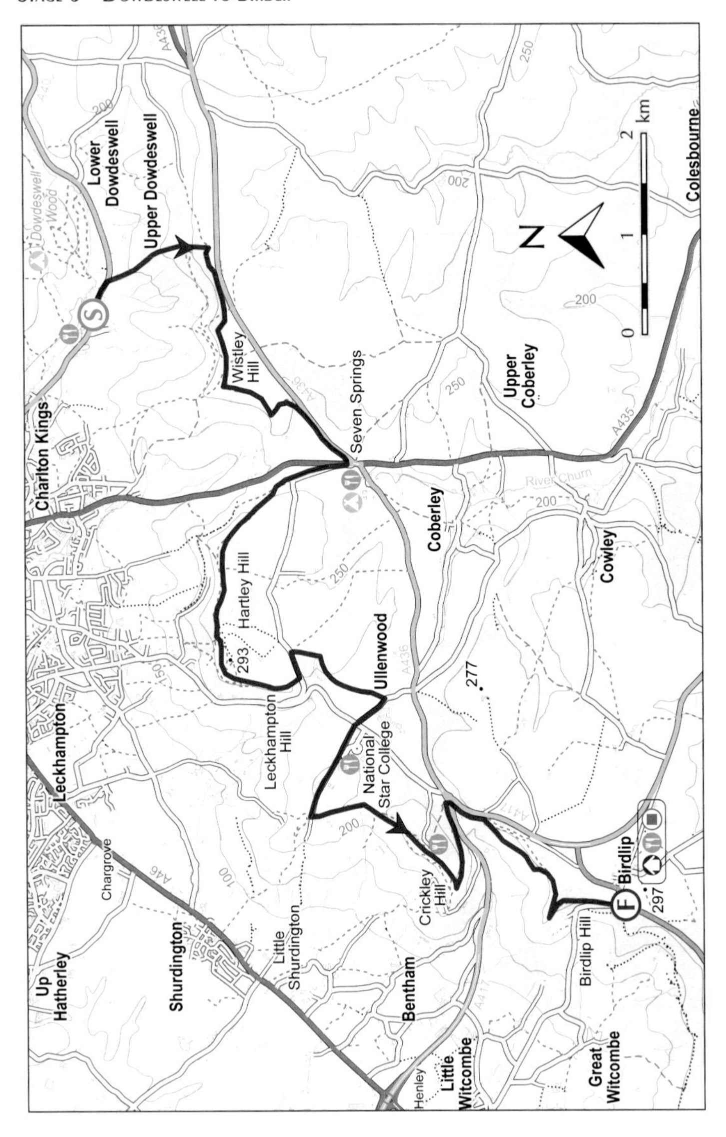
Lower Dowdeswell
Upper Dowdeswell
Dowdeswell Wood
A40
A436
Charlton Kings
Wistley Hill
Seven Springs
Upper Coberley
Colesbourne
A435
River Churn
Coberley
Cowley
Hartley Hill
293
Ullenwood
277
Leckhampton Hill
Leckhampton
National Star College
A417
Chargrove
A46
Shurdington
Little Shurdington
Crickley Hill
Birdlip
297
Birdlip Hill
Up Hatherley
Bentham
Henley
Little Witcombe
Great Witcombe
N
0
1
2
km

> The **Devil's Chimney** is a craggy finger of rock projecting from the scarp face terrace below Leckhampton Hill. The origin of the pinnacle is unclear, although it is thought that it was left by the 18th-century quarry workers as a joke. It survived an earthquake in 1926 and has since been repaired and protected from further damage.

Leckhampton Hill to Crickley Hill (5.5km, 1hr 20min)

The path turns south at Leckhampton Hill and continues along the edge to a parking area, descending all the way. Turn left up the road for 300 metres and turn right at the first track. Fork right here to descend past the substantial Salterley Grange and across fields with the Cotswold Hills Golf Club on the left. At the road, turn right to pass the **National Star College**. Refreshments are signed on the left at the far entrance.

Continue along the road and cross a busy road junction. The straight road ahead formerly led past a defence installation, but there is now a development of luxury houses. As the road descends, find a small set of steps on the left, just after a bridleway, signed for the CW to Crickley Hill, and take this path. The footpath runs parallel to the bridleway before entering the country park, which is a delightful wood with spring flowers growing abundantly. Follow this to a viewpoint, parking area and then the **Crickley Hill** visitor centre (refreshments, toilets and information). The main hill fort site is 250 metres further along, and is well explained in display boards.

Heading towards Crickley Hill on a good path

CRICKLEY HILL

Crickley was the site of around 15 separate periods of human activity, with strong evidence of occupation from as far back as 3700BC. There have been six major periods of activity here: the first Neolithic settlement, a causewayed enclosure dating from 3700BC; a second Neolithic settlement and evidence of a battle at around 3550BC; the construction of a cairn, long mound and sacred circle at around 2000BC; the first Iron Age hill fort at 700BC; the second Iron Age hill fort at 500BC; and various post-Roman settlements from AD420. The first Neolithic settlement occupied about 4 acres of the highest ground, surrounded by a double ring of banks and ditches. Further defensive measures followed, and the main rampart that survives to this day surrounded about 9 acres of hilltop and was initially constructed during the first Iron Age hill fort occupation.

Crickley Hill to Birdlip (3.6km, 1hr)

Walk through the Crickley Hill fort area, with fine views all around from this strong defensive position. At the end of the fort turn sharp left and head downhill, initially through open ground, then through a wooded enclosure (the Scrubbs) and then across a field to reach the roundabout, formerly the site of the well-known Air Balloon inn. Road widening works will cause re-routing and disruption for some years in this area, so look out for changes on the National Trail website and on the ground along the route.

Cross carefully and keep to the roadside alongside the A417 for 400 metres before branching right and climbing onto open ground with views back to Crickley Hill. Follow the path as it contours and enters woods, turning abruptly left at an area known as 'the Peak' before dropping down to meet the busy B4070 just below the village of Birdlip.

For the village, head carefully up the busy road, go round a sharp bend and find the Royal George hotel on the left. There are no other services in **Birdlip**, but its distance from Dowdeswell and Painswick means that many will stop here.

BIRDLIP

Birdlip (meaning 'a steep place') stands on the edge of the escarpment on the course of the Roman Ermin Street (or Way), which ran from Silcester (Calleva Atrebatum) via Cirencester (Corinium), where it crossed the Fosse Way, then on to Gloucester (Glevum). A similarly named Ermine Street (or Way), runs from London to Lincoln.

The Royal George Hotel at Birdlip welcomes CW walkers

NORTHBOUND FROM BIRDLIP TO DOWDESWELL (16.7km, 4hr 40min)

With no accommodation of any kind and only a couple of opportunities for refreshments, this stage runs through a mixture of woodlands, fields and elevated grassy hilltops with the most spectacular views. One of the highlights is passing through Crickley Hill Nature Reserve and the impressive hill fort site, followed by the airy hilltop and far-reaching views from Leckhampton Hill, with the Devil's Chimney just below, and Hartley Hill. A busy road intersection at Seven Springs is located just to the north of the possible source of the river Thames, then a climb over Wistley Hill leads through woods and fields to Dowdeswell.

Birdlip to Crickley Hill (3.6km, 1hr)

From the village descend the road with care and take the signed track on the right rising through woods to 'the Peak', turn sharply right and continue on an undulating route on the edge of the escarpment to eventually arrive at the A417. Turn left and walk beside the road to a busy road junction. Road widening works will cause rerouting and disruption for some years in this area, so look out for changes on the National Trail website and on the ground along the route. The path leads through woods known as the Scrubbs then climbs beside a stone wall onto the top of **Crickley Hill**. Turn sharply right and walk through the site of the hill fort then on to the Crickley Hill Country Park Nature Reserve visitor centre (refreshments, information and toilets).

Crickley Hill to Leckhampton Hill (5.5km, 1hr 20min)

The path now leads through the woods of the country park and through a narrow strip of woodland on the scarp edge. Turn right at the end onto a road past luxury houses, then cross straight over a crossroads and pass the **National Star College** (café) to reach a track on the left as the road bends right. Climb with a golf course on the right, then across fields to reach a road. Turn left, then after 300 metres turn right on a path to climb onto **Leckhampton Hill**. The Devil's Chimney is on a lower level just before reaching the main viewpoint.

Leckhampton Hill to Seven Springs (3.0km, 50min)

Continue on the path passing a trig point, then along the edge of the escarpment, curving right among woods and gorse. Head into an enclosed field, which leads on to a track then a road down to the **Seven Springs** roundabout. Refreshments are available at the Seven Springs pub just to the right across the road.

Seven Springs to Dowdeswell (4.6km, 1hr 30min)

Turn left over the A435 (before the roundabout), walk up the right margin of a field then up through woods and across fields onto **Wistley Hill**. Camping is available at Big Skies Glamping. The path continues on the scarp edge through and skirting woods, almost meeting the A436, then it breaks away to begin a sometimes steep descent through the ancient Lineover Wood and down to arrive at the A40 road at **Dowdeswell**.

STAGE 7

Birdlip to Painswick

Start	Road 5min below Birdlip
Finish	Painswick church
Distance	11.8km (7¼ miles)
Ascent	290m
Descent	400m
Time	3hr 30min
Refreshments	2 pubs, each 1km off route at Cranham Corner
Accommodation	Painswick, camping at Buckshead Farm

This is perhaps the most wooded stage of the CW. Descending from Birdlip, a bridleway is followed through Witcombe Wood under a canopy of trees, with bluebells and ramsons on the woodland floor during spring. The woods are mainly beech, with some ash, oak, whitebeam, wych elm and alder. The soft ground can get quite churned up and muddy, so be prepared in wet weather. Leading into Cooper's Hill Wood, the route passes Cooper's Hill, famed for the annual cheese-rolling event, into Buckholt Wood. Painswick Beacon is another hill fort with wide views just before the descent into the small town of Painswick.

Birdlip to Cooper's Hill (5.1km, 1hr 30min)

From Birdlip, descend the steep and busy B4070, taking as much care in your descent as was needed to climb the last 30 metres to Birdlip. For Buckshead Farm Campsite, it's probably best to head south on the B4070 for just under 2km. Turn left on the path which drops into the woods before turning left again. The track is good but hides a few very muddy sections; paths and tracks merge from either side but the CW is clear through **Witcombe Wood**. Various paths and tracks, some soft and muddy, lead through the woods, but National Trail waymarks always guide the way.

After 2km, the woods to the north abate and there are fine views over Witcombe Reservoir and Gloucester. A right turn leads to Cooper's Hill farm and the nearby remains of **Witcombe Roman Villa**, but continue ahead.

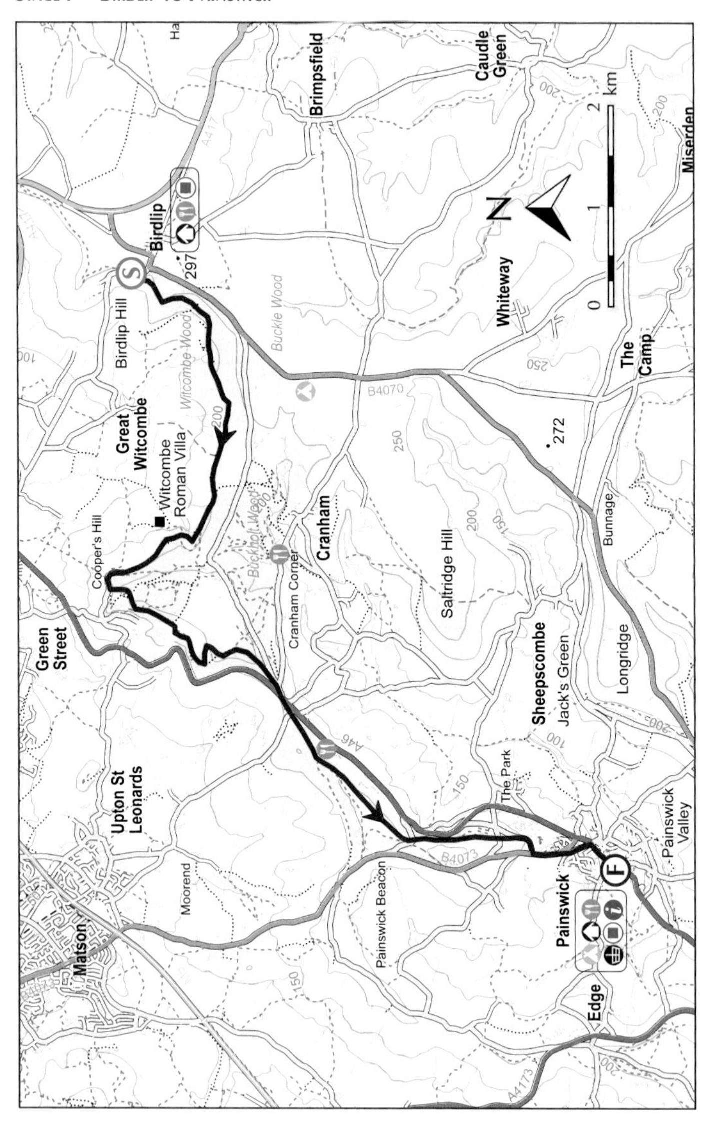
Birdlip
297
Brimpsfield
Caudle Green
Birdlip Hill
Witcombe Wood
Buckle Wood
Great Witcombe
Witcombe Roman Villa
Cooper's Hill
Buckholt Wood
Cranham Corner
Cranham
B4070
Whiteway
The Camp
Miserden
272
Saltridge Hill
Bunnage
Green Street
Sheepscombe
Jack's Green
Longridge
Upton St Leonards
A46
The Park
Painswick Valley
B4073
Moorend
Painswick Beacon
Painswick
Matson
Edge
A4173
A417
0
1
2 km
N
250
200
150
100

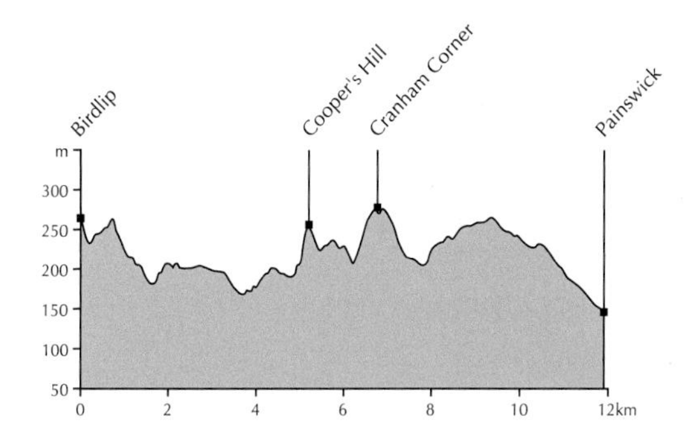

Witcombe Roman Villa dates from the first century AD and was built on land first exploited by Iron Age man. Excavations have unearthed sections of a bath house with fine mosaics depicting fish and seascapes. The villa is in the care of English Heritage, and is open throughout the year during daylight hours.

The track becomes a road. Pass cottages and swing left, soon under the unfeasibly steep slope of **Cooper's Hill** – it's hard to imagine chasing anything down it, except perhaps Double Gloucester cheese.

Cooper's Hill is not just a great viewpoint – it also forms part of the site of a large Iron Age encampment dating from 500BC. The hill's main claim to fame is for the annual festival of cheese-rolling, which takes place on its excessively steep (33%) grass slope. The origins of this ritual are not clear, but it is thought to have started as far back as 2000 years ago to maintain grazing rights, and there is evidence that it was an established ritual from around the 16th century. The festivities are held over the spring bank holiday each year, when contestants plunge heroically down the slope in pursuit of an 8lb (3kg) round Double Gloucester cheese, which the winner takes home as a prize. The 23-time men's race champion Chris Anderson retired after the 2022 race following a broken ankle and bruised ribs.

Head onwards and soon find a path that cuts back and steeply up to Cooper's Hill where you can inspect the slope from above. (On some maps, the route may avoid this – signs on the ground lead you up).

Cooper's Hill to Cranham Corner (2.3km, 45min)

From the hill follow a descending path back into woods. Brockworth Wood is followed by Upton Wood, and then **Buckholt Wood**, an important part of the Cotswold Commons and Beechwoods National Nature Reserve, noted for its beech and other trees, and for a range of over 780 species of wild fungi. Join a road and soon come to the junction with the A46, at **Cranham Corner**.

Refreshments are available off route at pubs along the A46 and in Cranham village (2km away). Camping can be found at Buckshead Farm Campsite 2km beyond Cranham.

Cranham Corner to Painswick (4.4km, 1hr 15min)

Continue past a parking area (with bench) and further into Buckholt Wood. The buildings of Prinknash Abbey and Park are below but hidden by trees. The path joins a road for 200 metres before continuing. (With 5 paths meeting here, keep a lookout for the signs; take the second path from the left.) Immediately come out onto the golf course and follow the well-made route alongside the course, passing under **Painswick Beacon** (283m) and its hill fort just above, which is easily accessible.

Painswick church and table-top tombs

Painswick Beacon has many other names: Painswick Hill (OS map), Kimsbury Castles, Castle Godwyn and Kimsbury Camp. Overlooking Gloucester and the Severn Vale, it was settled as Kimsbury Camp Hill Fort in the first century BC by late Iron Age tribes, and was used in Roman times and in 1052 as a temporary camp by Earl Godwyn (a Saxon leader in conflict with the Earl of Mercia), and again in 1643 by Royalist forces during the Siege of Gloucester. The 250 acres (101 hectares) of common land are speckled with birches and trim with the manicured greens and fairways of Painswick Hill Golf Club.

Cross an access road and pass alongside a quarry and stone cutting buildings, then continue descending across the golf course above the club house. Join a small road and then the larger B4073 and descend into **Painswick**, turning right down New Street to reach the fine church.

PAINSWICK

Painswick is a delightful old market town, but unlike the honey-gold of Chipping Campden, Painswick's stone is light grey in colour, making the buildings appear a little grander and more formal. Dating from the 13th century, New Street is one of the town's oldest streets, but other streets – especially those to the north-east of the church – are also worth exploring. Friday Street indicates the site of the Friday market, while Bisley Street – the original main street when Painswick was merely a village named Wicke – has a collection of splendid old buildings, which are among the oldest in the town. The old town stocks are located at the top of Hale Lane.

Painswick owes its elegance to the cloth trade, at the height of which 25 mills were powered by water from local streams. In the Civil War, Royalists attacked the town, damaging St Mary's Church with fire and cannonballs – the marks they left behind are evident to this day. The churchyard is noted for its clipped yew trees, its Renaissance-style table tombs and the lych gate with carvings of bells and music, made from the belfry roof timbers after the spire collapsed in 1883. The elegant 53m-high spire can be seen from a great distance.

Each September a clipping ceremony (based on the Saxon word for embracing, 'ycleping') takes place, in which the congregation joins hands to encircle the church while singing a special hymn.

The Tourist Information Centre is located in the churchyard and is open Monday to Friday from 10:00–16:00, and on Saturday from 10:00–13:00.

NORTHBOUND FROM PAINSWICK TO BIRDLIP (11.8km, 3hr 30min)

This stage enjoys upland hill forts and views with a mixture of woods and nature reserves. The initial climb out of Painswick and across a golf course leads to just below Painswick Beacon (283m), the impressive site of a hill fort with multiple ramparts. Pope's Wood follows, then along the scarp edge above Prinknash Abbey to Cranham Corner. After negotiating the busy road crossings, descend steps then into Buckholt Woods and Brockworth Woods – both National Nature Reserves – to arrive at the top of Cooper's Hill. Fine views from here, and down the precipitous 'cheese-rolling' slope. The onward path descends steeply to join a track, then continues into a continuous stretch of woodland comprising **Cooper's Wood**, Witcombe Wood and Birdlip Hill. The woods are mainly beech, with some ash, oak, whitebeam, wych elm and alder. The paths and tracks followed are soft underfoot, and are often flanked by ramsons, bluebells and other foliage; however, in wet conditions the soft ground can be quite muddy.

Painswick to Cranham Corner (4.4km, 1hr 15min)

Leave the town heading north up Gloucester Street, then take a narrow road to the right just past the last few houses. This leads uphill through a car park then through a gate onto a golf course. Following waymarks, continue ahead, rising steadily across the golf course. Pass beside a quarry/stoneworking plant then on a well-surfaced path just below **Painswick Beacon** to the end of the golf course where you enter Pope's Wood on a lane, then a track. This leads to **Cranham Corner**, a complicated series of crossing roads and tracks, but keep following National Trail signs.

Cranham Corner to Cooper's Hill (2.3km, 45min)

Having crossed the A46, enter Brockworth and Buckholt Woods and climb easily through these to emerge onto **Cooper's Hill**. Peer down the cheese-rolling slope ahead, then continue to the left, following markers steeply down and then to the right around the hill onto a lane, passing a row of cottages and houses.

Cooper's Hill to Birdlip (5.1km, 1hr 30min)

This final section of the stage is entirely through woods. Just past the cottages the metalled road ends; continue now on a track to enter Cooper's Wood. The way is always clearly marked as you negotiate crossing paths and tracks, undulating between around 150 and 250m for most of the way. Cooper's Wood seamlessly merges into **Witcombe Wood**. For Buckshead Farm Campsite, turn right in Witcombe Wood and climb steeply to the B4070. The route finally rises for the last time onto Birdlip Hill. The continuing route to Dowdeswell is immediately across the road. For overnight accommodation, turn up the often busy road to the right and walk into the village of **Birdlip**.

Looking down Cooper's Hill – even the keenest cheese-lover would tremble at the thought

STAGE 8

Painswick to Middleyard (King's Stanley)

Start	Painswick church
Finish	Middleyard
Distance	15.3km (9½ miles) (+2.8km (1¾ miles) via Selsley)
Ascent	300m
Descent	360m
Time	4hr 15min (+45min via Selsley)
Refreshments	Edgemoor Inn
Accommodation	Off route in Randwick, Stonehouse and Stroud, Selsley on alternative route, King's Stanley and Middleyard

This is a highly varied stage, with farmland, woodland, open edge and gentle sculpted woods before the route passes the sizeable town of Stroud, which intrudes little on the peaceful walk. There are a few options for the finish depending on accommodation, and this stage offers the only real route variant on the whole CW trail. The direct route, although quicker, is not as interesting as the variant via Selsley, Selsley Common and village are a delight and there's an excellent pub to visit. If combining this stage with Stage 7, the alternative route via Selsley Common (staying overnight in Selsley) makes for a very long and tiring option.

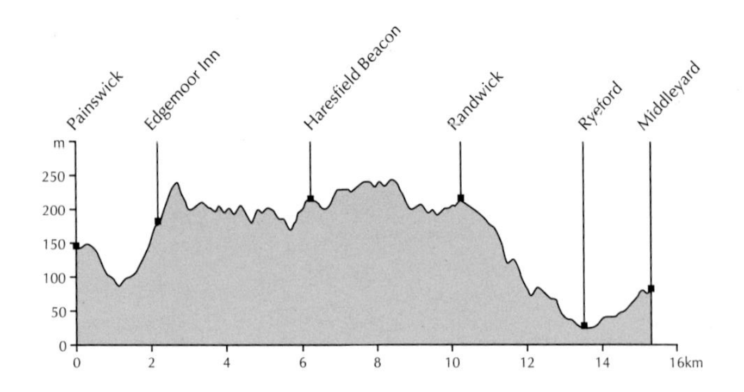

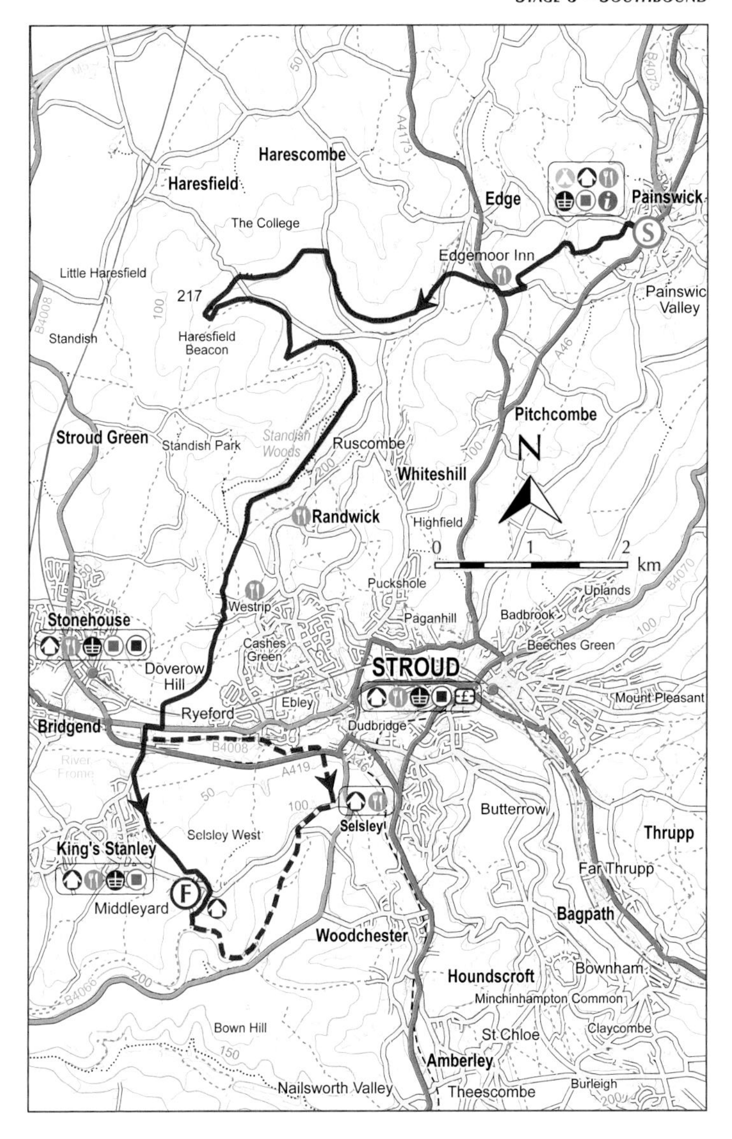
Harescombe
Haresfield
The College
Edge
Painswick
Edgemoor Inn
Little Haresfield
217
Painswick Valley
Standish
Haresfield Beacon
Pitchcombe
Stroud Green
Standish Park
Standish Woods
Ruscombe
Whiteshill
Randwick
Highfield
0
1
2
km
Puckshole
Uplands
Westrip
Paganhill
Badbrook
Stonehouse
Cashes Green
Beeches Green
Doverow Hill
STROUD
Ryeford
Ebley
Mount Pleasant
Bridgend
Dudbridge
River Frome
B4008
A419
Selsley
Butterrow
Selsley West
Thrupp
King's Stanley
Far Thrupp
Middleyard
Bagpath
Woodchester
Houndscroft
Bownham
Minchinhampton Common
Bown Hill
St Chloe
Claycombe
Amberley
Nailsworth Valley
Theescombe
Burleigh
A4173
A46
B4008
B4070
B4066
B4073

Painswick to Edgemoor Inn (2.2km, 45min)

From the church gate, head across the A46 (Stroud Road) onto Edge Road. After 250 metres turn left across a field to follow thin paths between substantial houses on a narrow lane. Descend to the stream with tennis courts to the left. Climb past houses (the first with what appears to be an elegant fireplace or door lintel on the external wall), then go left past farm buildings and climb through woods and into fields past the 'not the halfway point' marker. This 'not the halfway point' marker indicates 47 miles to Chipping Campden and 55 miles to Bath.

What appears to be an elegant fireplace built into the exterior wall

Turn left through a further field, then turn right up the steep Jenkin's Lane to a main road (A4173) and turn right to the **Edgemoor Inn** (refreshments). There are excellent views back to Painswick and its Beacon.

Edgemoor to Haresfield Beacon (4.0km, 1hr 10min)

Cross the road and climb through the uneven and folded ground of Rudge Hill Nature Reserve (a former quarry area) followed by a passage through Maitlands Wood. Descend a few steps and cross a road into woods, dropping down to the open bottom edge above farms and fields. Come to a road and head down for 300 metres before finding a turn left near a covered well. Continue through more woods. Again, the views are open past Cromwell's Stone. At the next road, turn left and immediately right to climb through woods then over open common to **Haresfield Beacon**. There are fine views east and south – the Black Mountains and Brecon Beacons are visible, and for the first time the Severn Bridges can be seen.

Haresfield Beacon is a splendid promontory viewpoint at the tip of Ring Hill, which is designated as a geological Site of Special Scientific Interest, notably for its Jurassic rocks. It is the site of a hill fort, and excavations at the eastern end of the hill in 1837 unearthed traces of a Roman building and a pot containing nearly 3000 coins.

Haresfield Beacon to Randwick (4.6km, 1hr 10min)

At the trig point turn sharply left and head along the grassy hillside and past Ring Hill hill fort. At a road, drop down to a lower path on steps and contour past woods to come to a wide common area. Keep right above the woods on faint paths to reach the splendid, but hard to use, contoured topograph. Turn left and reach a car park and road.

Here, turn right into the manicured **Standish Woods** on wide paths and follow the CW for 2km to emerge at a road above Randwick (accommodation). Standish Woods have a gentle, sculpted splendour and spring and summer flowers in abundance.

For **Randwick** turn left. At a junction turn left again for Randwick and right for the Carpenters Arms pub in **Westrip**. For accommodation, shops, refreshments and hotels in Stonehouse, turn right at the next road further down, or continue to Ryeford and follow roads into Stonehouse. The town of Stroud (formerly a centre of the wool trade) and surrounding villages are spread out below. The route makes a grassy descent through fields and past a vineyard into Ryeford to reach the Stroudwater Canal.

Randwick to Ryeford (2.5km, 40min)

From the road continue ahead down the fields of Maiden Hill. Follow the CW left to cross a second road then drop down to a third. Turn right and then left in 100 metres, descending initially through fields before passing a well-established

Looking over Stroud and surrounding villages on the descent from Randwick

vineyard. Cross the railway on a bridge, then pass sports fields. At a road (the B4008) turn right under a footbridge and past a school, and then turn left at a small roundabout to reach the **Ryeford Bridge** and Stroudwater Canal.

The **Stroudwater Canal** was opened in 1779 to service the industrialised Stroud Valley. It was only 8 miles (12.5km) long, but it linked Stroud town with the navigable River Severn at Upper Framilode by way of a dozen locks.

Ryeford to King's Stanley and Middleyard (2.0km, 30min)

Continue down and cross the busy A419 at the lights. Continue ahead, passing the bulk of the Stanley Mills (a substantial red building – now being conserved) and after 500 metres take the CW south to the left into fields. Climb gently with **King's Stanley** to the right and after a short section on narrow paths (or a shorter section of road) bear left again into fields and climb steadily to **Middleyard**.

Accommodation, shops and other facilities are available in King's Stanley and Middleyard.

Alternative route – Ryeford to Selsley and Middleyard (5.4km, 1hr 40min)

This route allows accommodation in Selsley (or Stroud) to be reached. At the Ryeford Bridge turn left along the disused but pleasant canal. After 20min, turn right and cross fields to walk alongside the A419. At a road crossing before a roundabout, cross the road and climb through steepening fields to **Selsley**. The Bell Inn (accommodation, refreshments) is 300 metres off route to the left.

The onward route turns right and passes Selsley church before turning left onto Selsley Common. It's a steep climb to the summit of the long ridge extending southwards from Stroud. Continue down the ridge, which is much gentler on this side, and into woods. After 20min reach the path junction in Pen Wood near **Middleyard**.

For Middleyard turn right and drop down for 400 metres into the village. For the onward route to Dursley keep ahead on the CW (see Stage 9).

NORTHBOUND FROM KING'S STANLEY AND MIDDLEYARD TO PAINSWICK (15.3km, 4hr 30min)

This is a lovely stage of the route, combining woods and viewpoints with meadows and a sheltered stream valley before a final short ascent into Painswick. Crossing fields from Middleyard to reach Stanley Mill and the Stroudwater Canal (where the alternative route via Selsley and Selsley Common rejoins), the way climbs again through a vineyard and up into Standish Woods, then onto Haresfield Beacon, one of the best CW viewpoints. Continuing on through more woods, the route descends then climbs again to reach the Edgemoor Inn. It then continues down over more meadows, over a stream and up to the market town of Painswick.

The alternative route from just above Middleyard leads through woods and up onto Selsley Common, then down to the village of Selsley (accommodation). The route continues down across fields then along the Stroudwater Canal.

Middleyard to Ryeford (2km, 30min)

From the junction of paths above **Middleyard**, drop down between a few houses and across fields to Middleyard, then go right by the old Baptist church and over more fields, passing **King's Stanley** on the left, to reach a road heading north. Turn right, passing Stanley Mill. Cross the busy A419 over the Stroudwater Canal, then go right at the next road. After 500 metres turn left onto a path just after a dental surgery.

Ryeford to Randwick (2.5km, 50min)

The route climbs steadily over the railway and through a vineyard, then across fields. At the first road turn right then left (or, for refreshments, turn right and then head up to the left for the Carpenters Arms). For accommodation and refreshments at Randwick, continue past the Carpenters Arms then on a rising road to **Randwick**.

Randwick to Haresfield Beacon (4.6km, 1hr 20min)

At the next road turn left then immediately right through a small wood, then go straight ahead at a small road and parking area into the beautiful and well-managed **Standish Woods**. After 2km turn left towards **Haresfield Beacon** at a car park. Cross open common land leading directly to Haresfield and fine views.

Fine views from Haresfield Beacon

Haresfield Beacon to Edgemoor Inn (4.0km, 1hr 10min)
From the trigpoint, turn sharply right over soft grass then into woods, keeping mainly to or near the scarp edge. Enjoy more fine views then drop to a minor road. Turn left then immediately right to continue through more woods, passing Cromwell's Stone, then go down to a minor road by cottages and a covered well. Turn right up the road for 300 metres, then branch left on a track through more woods. Climb steeply to cross a road, then continue over lumpy (formerly quarried) ground to the A4173. Cross to the **Edgemoor Inn** (refreshments).

Edgemoor Inn to Painswick (2.2km, 40min)
Just beyond the Edgemoor Inn car park, descend steeply down Jenkin's Lane. Turn left then right across fields and head down past the old 'halfway' marker to woods and over a stream at Washbrook Farm. Now climb again across a series of fields with tennis courts to the right to meet Edge Road. Turn right and walk into the centre of **Painswick**, with its fine church immediately ahead.

STAGE 9

Middleyard (King's Stanley) to Dursley

Start	Middleyard
Finish	Dursley market
Distance	10.8km (6¾ miles)
Ascent	410m
Descent	420m
Time	3hr 15min
Refreshments	None
Accommodation	None until Dursley, camping at Nympsfield (off route)

Although shorter than some, this stage involves a fair amount of climbing and descending. It could be combined with Stage 8, making a full – but not excessively long – day, or it could be extended to either North Nibley or even Wotton-under-Edge (leaving the walker well placed to reach Bath in a further two days). There are no refreshments of any kind on this stage so make sure you have adequate supplies. This is another mainly wooded stage, with interest provided by Nympsfield Long Barrow and an option to visit another long barrow at Hetty Pegler's Tump. The impressive Uley Bury Hill Fort is worth a minor detour. A steep climb onto the outlying hills of Cam Long Down and Cam Peak is rewarded with long views, before a gentle and mellow route across fields to the bustling market town of Dursley.

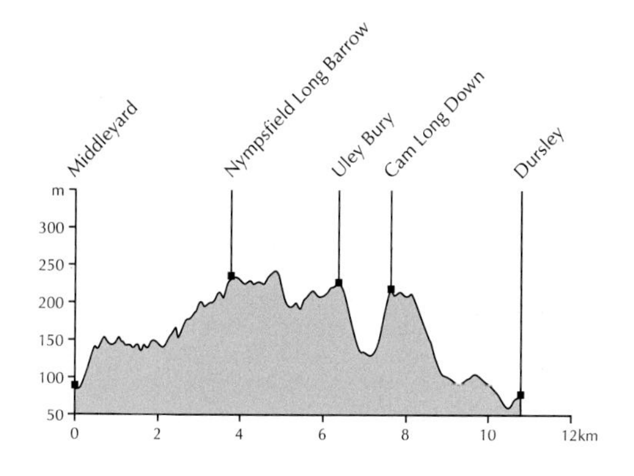

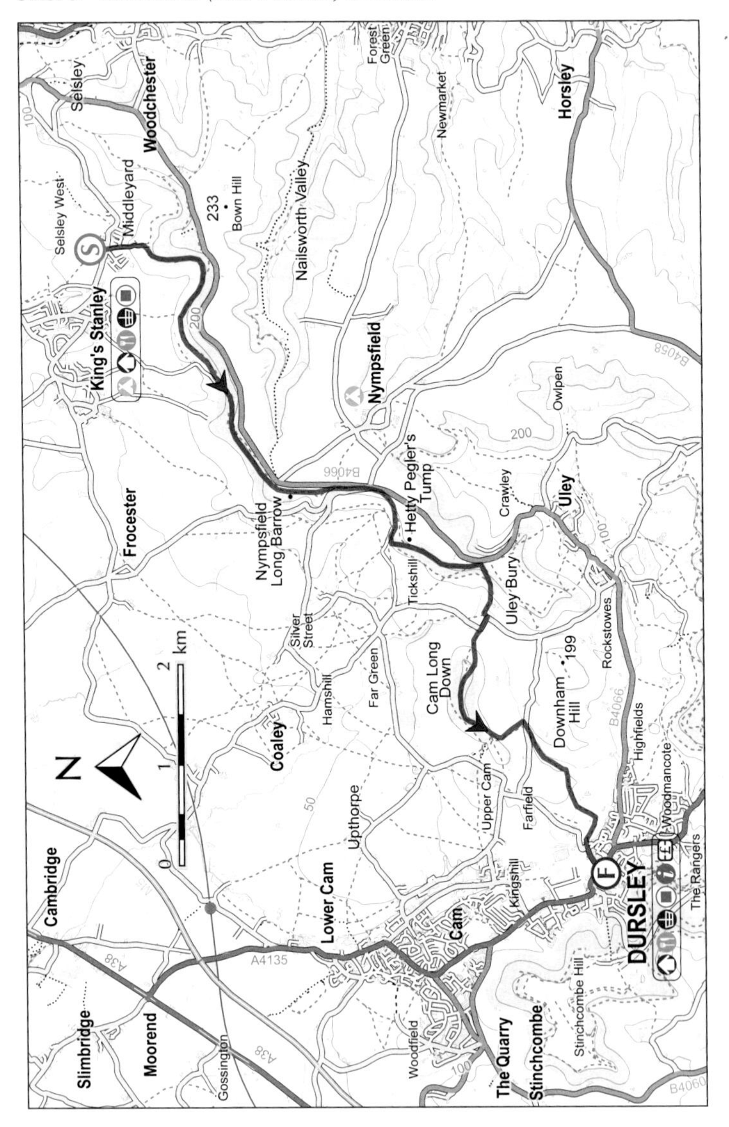
Selsley
Woodchester
Forest Green
Newmarket
Horsley
Selsley West
Middleyard
233
Bown Hill
Nailsworth Valley
King's Stanley
200
Nympsfield
B4058
Frocester
Nympsfield Long Barrow
B4066
Hetty Pegler's Tump
Owlpen
200
Crawley
Uley
Tickshill
Uley Bury
100
Silver Street
N
0
1
2
km
Far Green
Cam Long Down
Downham Hill
199
Rockstowes
Hamshill
Coaley
B4066
Highfields
Upthorpe
50
Upper Cam
Farfield
Woodmancote
Cambridge
Lower Cam
Kingshill
DURSLEY
The Rangers
M5
A38
A4135
Cam
Stinchcombe Hill
Slimbridge
Moorend
Woodfield
The Quarry
Stinchcombe
Gossington
A38
100
B4060

Middleyard to Nympsfield Long Barrow (3.8km, 1hr 15min)

Most of this section is in fine beech woods – Pen Wood, Stanley Wood and Buckholt Wood – with spring and summer flowers. From the converted baptist church in Middleyard, continue uphill on a road and turn right on a smaller road. After 100 metres, keep ahead on a track where the road turns left. Climb the track and then fields to meet another road. Turn left and climb to the well-signed junction of paths where the Selsley alternative rejoins this main route.

Turn right and continue in woods, occasionally muddy. The path keeps to the bottom of the woods so there are good views back to King's Stanley. Pass above farms, one with a substantial tower attached and, after a little over an hour, emerge into an open area with picnic tables and parking. The reconstructed **Nympsfield Long Barrow** is ahead.

Nympsfield Long Barrow is similar in concept to many Neolithic barrows of the Cotswold–Severn Group. Constructed about 5500 years ago, it was used for burials, and was probably also a place of ritual which was used to mark territory. Originally the mound stood about 2m high and was edged with drystone walling. The scattered remains of 20 people, together with a flint arrowhead and some pottery, were discovered during a 1937 excavation. The barrow was used for about two centuries, after which the forecourt was filled with stone. The site was first excavated in 1862, and in 1974 it was reconstructed to the form seen today.

Nympsfield Long Barrow to Uley Bury Hill Fort (2.5km 45min)

Continue through the grassy area with picnic tables scattered about and pass a viewpoint and topograph with excellent views over the Severn valley and to the Welsh mountains in the distance. Keep ahead and pass through an abandoned quarry and climb out on steps to come to a busy road junction by Coaley Wood. Cross with care and keep to the roadside for 50 metres before dropping down again into the wood. (**Hetty Pegler's Tump** is 500 metres further along the road).

Hetty Pegler's Tump is a Neolithic burial mound found just off the route. Measuring 42 metres long by 27 metres wide, the covering mound is about 3 metres high. From a long internal passageway, there are two pairs of side chambers and a single chamber at the western end. The two northern chambers have been sealed off. Excavations have unearthed pieces of Roman pottery and an Edward IV silver groat. The mound gained its curious name because it stands on land that was owned by Henry and Hester (or Hetty) Pegler during the 17th century.

Descend quite steeply and follow the path through woods before a gradual climb to a path junction close by the B4066. **Uley Bury** is 2min walk ahead, with information boards. A full circuit takes about 30min.

> **Uley Bury Hill Fort** occupies an enormous area of more than 30 acres (12 hectares) and is almost entirely protected by the 90m steep sides of the edge of the escarpment south-east of Cam Long Down. Dating from the Iron Age, it is certainly an impressive site. A ditch and rampart complete the defences. Uley Bury has never been excavated, although second- and fourth-century Roman coins have been found here.

Uley Bury Hill Fort to Dursley (4.5km, 1hr 15min)

From the path junction, turn right on a path that descends steeply, soon passing Hodgecombe Farm. Continue on the drive and come to a small road. Turn right, and after 100 metres turn left into a field to pass farm buildings. Start to climb, ever steeper, and pass through a stile to reach the summit of **Cam Long Down**. It's surprising that no hill fort is identified here – it's a naturally fortified position. The bluebell-covered slopes make a fine descent before you drop down through pastures and into the old wool town of Dursley.

Looking ahead to the stiff climb up Cam Long Down

Approaching the centre of Dursley with the market directly ahead

Head along the ridge and soon descend. (Camp Peak, lower than the main summit, is ahead and makes for a worthwhile detour.) Cross a path junction and come almost immediately to another. Turn right and then left after 50 metres to descend a field to a road.

Cross the road and follow the path between houses and by a stream. The onward path crosses a field and keeps to the edge of the next one. Emerge above the substantial Chestal House. Bear left through a field and, at the house driveway, turn right. Follow the drive to a road and turn left past a bowling club. Pass houses and apartment buildings, come to a road and cross it, taking Long Street into the centre of **Dursley**.

Pass the church on the left. The town museum (Heritage Centre) is to the right, while the prominent market is across the street where there are cafés and shops.

There are no facilities on this stage until you reach Dursley, which has accommodation, cafés, pubs, shops and a supermarket.

NORTHBOUND FROM DURSLEY TO MIDDLEYARD (KING'S STANLEY) (10.8km, 3hr 30min)

This stage begins with a gentle route across fields before climbing steeply onto the outlying ridge of Cam Long Down, with fine views. An even steeper descent from the ridge briefly crosses farmland before the climb to Uley Bury Hill Fort. The route then continues mainly through woods undulating on the edge of the escarpment. Passing Nympsfield Long Barrow, the way continues through more woods to a point just above Middleyard, where the Cotswold Way has two alternatives. There are no facilities on this stage.

Dursley to Uley Bury Hill Fort (4.5km, 1hr 30min)

From the market hall, take Long Street to the left of the church, pass apartment buildings, then take the rising track past the bowling club and follow it to the right through woods. Turn left into a field, passing Chestal House. Then head right below a rounded hill and down beside a stream to reach a small road and path junctions. Take the clear path rising on the right edge of a field with Cam Peak ahead, then head right up onto **Cam Long Down**. At the far eastern end of Cam Long Down descend steeply, heading directly towards farm buildings, then maintain this direction onto a road, turn left onto a track past Hodgecombe Farm and climb steeply to the top of the escarpment by a bench seat near a road. **Uley Bury Hill Fort** is just to the right.

Uley Bury Hill Fort to Nympsfield Long Barrow (2.5km, 45min)

Descending a little through Coaley Wood, pass below the site of **Hetty Pegler's Tump** (a long barrow), then rise to keep parallel with the road. Cross a busy road at an awkward 'Y' junction and drop down through an old quarry before emerging from the woods to an open area with **Nympsfield Long Barrow** on the left, with picnic tables and a parking area.

Nympsfield Long Barrow to Middleyard (3.8km, 1hr 15min)

The route now enters Buckholt Wood and descends almost to the bottom of the steepest scarp slope to pass through, then below, Stanley Wood, now with views across to King's Stanley and Middleyard. Re-entering woods, the line of the lower escarpment is followed to reach a path junction indicating a route via Middleyard, or an alternative route east via Selsley.

Nympsfield Long Barrow

Descend an enclosed track then head right across a sloping field to another track leading to a road. Turn left and continue through the village of **Middleyard** to a road junction with a Baptist church on the right.

STAGE 10

Dursley to Wotton-under-Edge

Start	Market in Dursley
Finish	Church in Wotton-under-Edge
Distance	12.5km (7¾ miles) (4km less if taking shortcut at golf course)
Ascent	295m
Descent	270m
Time	3hr 30min (1hr less if taking shortcut at golf course)
Refreshments	Stinchcombe Golf Course, Black Horse Inn in North Nibley
Accommodation	North Nibley and Wotton-under-Edge

This stage is punctuated by two distinct phases of ascent and descent. There are woods to walk through, but there are also broad, grassy scarp edge views to enjoy, especially from the Drakestone Point on Stinchcombe Hill and the Tyndale Monument on Nibley Knoll. Westridge Wood is crossed on forest tracks, and some route diversions may be needed when forestry work is taking place. Stinchcombe Golf Course is circumnavigated on the full route, dropping in and out of woods on the edge, and there is a good view from Drakestone Point. If you are combining this stage with Stage 9, there is an option to reduce the overall time by about 1 hour by taking the shorter CW route directly across Stinchcombe Hill Golf Course.

From North Nibley to Wotton-under-Edge is a Cotswold Way 'in miniature' section, which has one of nearly everything that the CW offers. The steep climb to Tyndale's Tower (commemorating the early 16th-century Bible translator) is followed by striding out over the grasslands of Nibley Knoll. Traverse Westridge Wood, recently disturbed by forestry operations, and pass the site of a hill fort before descending past a small plantation, with views over Wotton and a sharp drop into the town.

Dursley to Stinchcombe Hill Golf Course (5.4km, 1hr 30min)

From the market in the centre of Dursley, follow the shopping street – Parsonage Street – and turn left at the junction onto Hay Lane. Pass the rather unexpected modernist library and curve right past the Old Spot Inn into Hill Street, which does exactly what it promises. Climb steeply and, where the road turns left, continue

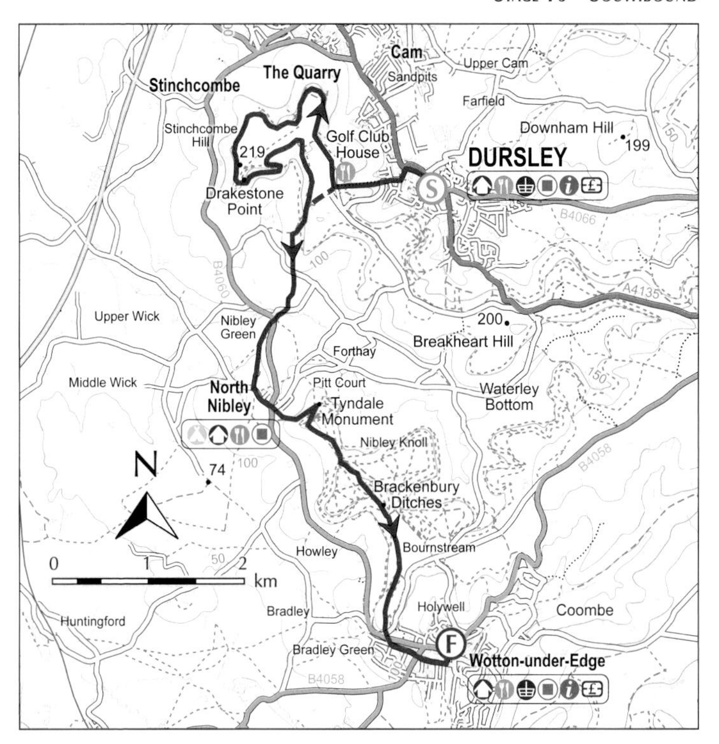
Cam
Upper Cam
The Quarry
Sandpits
Stinchcombe
Farfield
Stinchcombe Hill
Golf Club House
Downham Hill
199
219
DURSLEY
Drakestone Point
B4066
100
B4060
A4135
Upper Wick
Nibley Green
200
Breakheart Hill
Forthay
Middle Wick
Pitt Court
North Nibley
Tyndale Monument
Waterley Bottom
150
Nibley Knoll
B4058
N
74
100
Brackenbury Ditches
Howley
Bournstream
0
1
2
km
50
Huntingford
Bradley
Holywell
Coombe
Bradley Green
Wotton-under-Edge
B4058

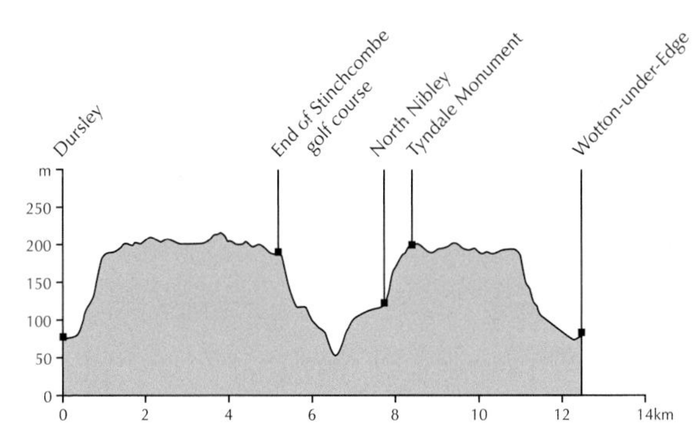
Dursley
End of Stinchcombe golf course
North Nibley
Tyndale Monument
Wotton-under-Edge
m
250
200
150
100
50
0
0
2
4
6
8
10
12
14km

ahead on the CW track and climb more to reach the golf course and its clubhouse (refreshments) to the right. Here there are two alternatives. Either a short walk across to continue to North Nibley, or an hour-long tour of the edges. Your choice may depend on the weather and your plans for the day.

For the short route, turn left to pass a parking area and follow CW signs across the course. As the path starts to drop, the longer route meets from the right.

For the longer route, turn right and follow CW signs across the course. Soon the path starts to run at the edge of the course, dipping in and out of woods and the steep edge. Follow this round several promontories and bays to reach **Drakestone Point**, with a trig point and more fine views. Continue around the course, past a parking area and meet the shortcut where the path begins to drop.

Stinchcombe Hill is a magnificent vantage point, with a topograph near Drakestone Point highlighting some of the main features in the panorama. These include Berkeley Castle, the Malvern Hills, the Brecon Beacons, and even Exmoor, which – it is claimed – can be seen from here.

Making a circuit of Stinchcombe Hill, one of the world's first Friendship Trails has been waymarked to form a link between the CW and the Jeju Olle trail on Jeju Island off the south-west coast of Korea – a UNESCO World Heritage Site. Special signs have been added to selected Cotswold Way marker posts.

Stinchcombe Hill to North Nibley (2.4km, 45min)

Drop down the steep path and turn left to cross gas pipelines by a bridge. The substantial Tyndale Monument is visible for most of the route, perched 80m above North Nibley. Continue through fields to meet Park Lane, turn left and then immediately right into a large and often cropped field (muddy if wet), and drop again to reach a narrow lane near houses. Turn right and continue past the bridge over the attractive Doverte Brook with old mill houses, then rise to reach a road junction. Take a lane directly across and follow this to **North Nibley**. Turn left on the road and continue to reach the Black Horse Inn (accommodation, refreshments).

North Nibley means 'the clearing near the peak'. Among its oldest dwellings is Nibley House, which was partially rebuilt in 1763 from an earlier house. Just beyond Nibley House is the Church of St Martin, which dates from the 15th century.

Nearby is Nibley Green, where the last battle to be fought in England between private armies took place in 1470, between the Berkeleys and the Lisles. About 2000 men took part and Lord Lisle, who had challenged Lord Berkeley to do battle over the ownership of Berkeley Castle, was shot first in

Heading across arable fields with North Nibley on the horizon

the face then stabbed to death. His retainer army fled and was scattered over the surrounding countryside, while his house was sacked by Berkeley's men. Around 150 men died in this senseless conflict.

North Nibley to Wotton-under-Edge (4.7km, 1hr 15min)

From the Black Horse Inn, head uphill past houses and turn left on a track. This sunken track rises through woods before turning right after 10min of uphill work to approach the **Tyndale Monument**. It is free to enter; the solid steps inside are slightly enclosing, and there are just over 200 of them to the top where there are even better views.

The **Tyndale Monument** on Nibley Knoll is a prominent landmark that can be seen from a great distance. Standing 34m high, it was designed by SS Teulon and was erected in 1866 in memory of William Tyndale, who translated the Bible into English. It is believed that Tyndale was born at or near North Nibley in 1484. Condemned as a heretic, he was strangled and burned in Flanders on 6 October 1536. His English translation of the New Testament is extensively in the King James Bible of 1611. The tower is open all year.

Continue across the open common of Nibley Knoll and merge with other paths to enter Westridge Wood. Turn right and pass by the site of **Brackenbury Ditches** fort. There are many paths joining and leaving the CW route, so watch the waymarks. Emerge from the wood by the side of a large flat field before starting to descend.

Brackenbury Ditches is the name given to another Iron Age hill fort, which is rather overgrown with trees, but not entirely hidden. The outer defensive ditch has been cleared but, presumably because of the dense woodland cover within, the site has never been excavated. Nearby, at a junction of paths in Westridge Wood, the outlawed practice of cockfighting used to take place.

Pass to the left of a clump of trees surrounded by a circular wall – this small grove of trees, which has been replanted several times, is known as the Jubilee Plantation. There are excellent views over the town and the hills for the next stage.

The **Jubilee Plantation** was initially planted to celebrate the Duke of Wellington's victory over Napoleon at Waterloo in 1815, but the trees were felled for a bonfire to mark the end of the Crimean War. The circular wall was built and more trees were planted in 1887 to celebrate Queen Victoria's golden jubilee. Yet more planting took place in 1952.

Keep heading down and come to a road (the B4060). Turn left and then right on Bradley Street, and follow the road down into the centre of **Wotton-under-Edge**. At a crossroads the road becomes High Street. Pass shops then follow a circuitous route past old village houses to come to the church.

The elegant church in Wotton marks the start of the next stage

NORTHBOUND FROM WOTTON-UNDER-EDGE TO DURSLEY (12.5km, 3hr 30min)

This lovely stage can easily be shortened if time is short or bad weather makes the circuit of Stinchcombe Hill unrewarding. Climbing out of Wotton-under-Edge, pass the Jubilee Plantation on Wotton Hill, then the route continues up onto open grassland at the top of the escarpment. The way through Westridge Wood may have forestry diversions to watch for, then the route emerges onto a sloping grassy expanse heading directly to the Tyndale Monument. A sunken lane leads to North Nibley, then head down through lanes and across fields to rise again onto Stinchcombe Hill. From the golf clubhouse, a lane descends through woods leading directly down into Dursley.

Wotton-under-Edge to North Nibley (4.7km, 1hr 25min)

From the church, follow signs between buildings to reach a road junction by the war memorial. Cross to Church Street, then turn right up Long Street, with the main shops and cafés on either side. Continue north up Bradley Street then, at the edge of the town, branch right onto a steep path and climb through trees to reach the Jubilee Plantation on Wotton Hill, with great views back down to Wotton-under-Edge.

Now on the scarp edge, enjoy 15min striding out with grassy turf to your right along the edge of woods, then pass through Westridge Wood. Forest tracks criss-cross the woods, and it may be necessary to follow diversions when there are forestry works. To the left is **Brackenbury Ditches** – another hill fort hidden in the trees. Emerging from the woods, climb easily across grassy common land directly to the **Tyndale Monument**.

The Tyndale Monument is open to the public but has over 200 enclosed steps to climb

Looking down over North Nibley from the Tynedale Monument

After enjoying the views – which are even more extensive if you climb the tower – turn right, keeping woods on your left, then after 200 metres turn down into the woods then turn left onto a sunken lane. At the bottom of the lane turn right into **North Nibley**, with the Black Horse Inn (accommodation, refreshments) seen directly ahead.

North Nibley to Stinchcombe Golf Course (2.4km, 40min)

With your back to the Black Horse Inn, cross over the main road (B4060) and, at a small, grassy triangle, turn right onto a lane. North Nibley House and church are to the left. The lane leads gradually more steeply down to cross the B4060 again. Continue directly ahead past a few houses and over a stream. Fork left onto a path rising across a large field. At the next narrow road turn left then immediately right, then climb steeply through woods to arrive at the edge of a golf course on Stinchcombe Hill and a choice of routes.

Stinchcombe Golf Course to Dursley (5.4km, 1hr 25min)

The main route now turns left to follow the edge of the golf course, dipping briefly in and out of woods on the scarp edge, to **Drakestone Point**, then it continues in much the same way to eventually reach the Stinchcombe Golf Clubhouse (refreshments).

Cotswold Way signs also indicate a direct route straight across the golf course to the clubhouse, and this is recommended if visibility is poor or if time is short. This saves 1hr and 4km.

A track to the right of the clubhouse descends through woods to meet the aptly named Hill Road which leads directly down into **Dursley**. Pass the modern library and information building on the left, then turn right along a pedestrianised high street to the old market square.

STAGE 11

Wotton-under-Edge to Hawkesbury Upton

Start	Church in Wotton-under-Edge
Finish	Hawkesbury Upton
Distance	11.6km (7¼ miles)
Ascent	390m
Descent	300m
Time	3hr 30min
Refreshments	None until Hawkesbury Upton
Accommodation	None until Petty France, 2km off route at Hawkesbury Upton

This stage is where the nature of the Cotswold Way seems to change, becoming a little more mellow. There are plenty of hills to climb; however, the route now passes through more valleys and undulating uplands. A climb and tour of the edges above Wotton leads to a deeply sunken lane down from the escarpment to the mill villages of Wortley, Alderley and Kilcott, then up again and across high fields to the Somerset Monument on the outskirts of Hawkesbury Upton. This stage can be combined with Stage 12 where there are good accommodation options in or near Tormarton.

Wotton-under-Edge to Alderley (5.9km, 1hr 45min)

From St Mary the Virgin Church, head out of Wotton and take the second small lane, Valley Road, between houses. Drop to a path by a stream and continue along this, crossing a road to reach another (Combe Lane). Turn right and, where the road bends right, turn left and then immediately right to find a steeply climbing path into woods. Meet a road (Blackquarries Hill) and turn left, continuing to climb. Follow this for 15min and look out for a signed track doubling back right.

Take this and continue for 500 metres, taking a path into a field. Signs appear to point down, but it is much better to turn left and stay high in the field before re-joining the lane after 400 metres. Keep to this lane, which heads into the lightly wooded Wortley Hill before dropping down, crossing many forestry tracks. The path becomes a deeply sunken lane before popping out near the buildings of **Wortley** and Elmtree Farm.

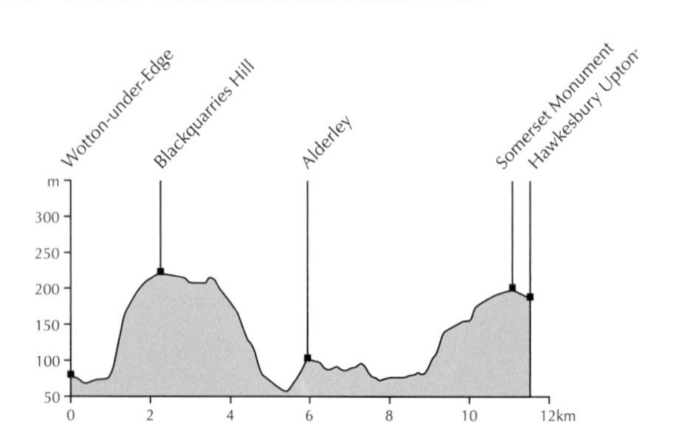

Continue across the road and bear left through the field to cross a stream by a bridge. Bear right on a track which climbs gradually to the next hamlet, which is **Alderley**.

Wortley and Alderley both had cloth mills powered by the local streams. Wortley is famed as the birthplace of Stephen Hopkins, who made his fortune in the cloth trade and then sailed to America with the Pilgrim Fathers in 1620, where he became an important official and died there in 1644.

Alderley is 'the clearing in the alders', a hamlet set on a spur of land between the Ozleworth and Kilcott valleys. The village was home to Lord Chief Justice Matthew Hale (1609–76), who served Charles I, Cromwell's Protectorate and later under Charles II, the botanical artist Marianne North (died 1890) and another eminent botanist, Brian Houghton Hodgson, who lived for a while at the Grange.

Heading across fields between Wortley and Alderley

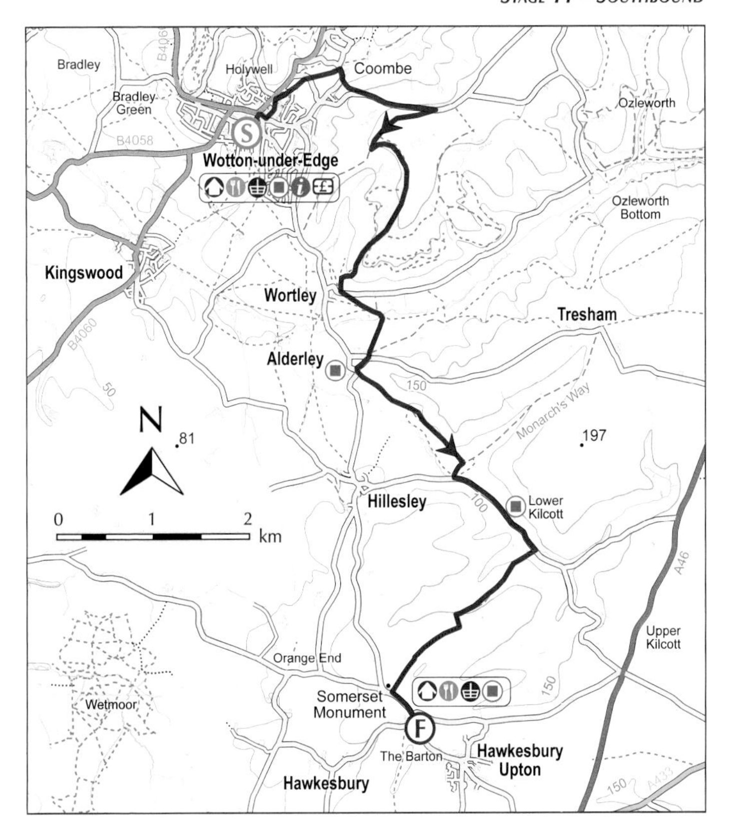

Alderley to Hawkesbury Upton (5.7km, 1hr 45min)

Continue ahead on a road through Alderley. Pass the fine old church and turn left onto a track. This follows the field boundary. After 20min turn right on a track and left on a minor road near Kilcott Mill. Take the road for 15min past the fish farm ponds at **Lower Kilcott**. Several paths head off to the right; take the third one with CW signage and climb a lane into a wood. Continue through fields and through Claypit Wood. Bear left then right along a field side path with the **Somerset Monument** directly ahead. Turn left along the road. The trail continues south to the right at Home Farm.

The stream at Lower Kilcott

The **Somerset Monument** was built in 1846 in memory of General Lord Somerset, a son of the fifth Duke of Beaufort, whose family seat was at nearby Badminton, of horse trials fame. General Somerset served in the army from 1793, including in the Peninsular War and the War of the Seventh Coalition, and under Wellington at the Battle of Waterloo. He was awarded a GCB (Grand Cross Star of the Most Honourable Order of the Bath) in 1834. He was MP for Cirencester between 1834 and 1837. The tower stands more than 30m high and has a viewing platform. It is also known as the Hawkesbury Monument.

Hawkesbury Upton village is 500 metres ahead with refreshments, accommodation and a small shop.

HAWKESBURY UPTON

Hawkesbury Upton developed around a farm mentioned in a document of AD972, but has grown very little since. The village street is lined with houses of a similar age, with a pub, village shop and primary school. An annual horticultural show held in late August has run continuously since 1885.

NORTHBOUND FROM HAWKESBURY UPTON TO WOTTON-UNDER-EDGE

(11.6km, 3hr 10min)

This is another stage full of interest and varied landscapes. Beginning high on the escarpment past the Somerset Monument, the route crosses fields and heads through woods before descending into the Kilcott Valley, with its fish farm, former mill and occasional mill ponds and streams. The path then climbs a little above the valley and across fields to reach Alderley, then Wortley, before climbing up on a sunken lane and through woods to regain the scarp edge, eventually joining a minor road and taking a sharp turn left. A steep descent on a path then a series of village roads leads into Wotton-under-Edge to arrive at the church.

Hawkesbury Upton to Alderley (5.7km, 1hr 30min)

From the pond on the edge of the village, follow the road around a bend to the **Somerset Monument** then take the route past a lodge cottage along a track across Clay Hill. Turn left down into Claypit Wood and then turn right to descend and reach a road opposite cottages in **Lower Kilcott**. Turn left following the road and Kilcott stream past a fish farm and mill, then after 1km turn right on a track. Shortly after turn left across a series of fields, keeping just above the Kilcott Valley to reach **Alderley**.

Alderley to Wotton-under-Edge (5.9km, 1hr 40min)

From the church turn right, then at the next road junction continue directly ahead onto a lane leading directly to a track. Cross a stream, then go across two fields to reach **Wortley**. Pass straight through the hamlet then up an ancient sunken lane through woods leading up onto the escarpment. Keep to the scarp edge (signs direct the CW left, briefly down through more woods, then up to rejoin the escarpment) and continue to reach a small road. Turn sharply left along the road, then branch right onto a steep path through woods to join another road. Cross a stream and immediately turn left to follow the stream, crossing another road to arrive at the Church of St Mary the Virgin in **Wotton-under-Edge**.

STAGE 12

Hawkesbury Upton to Tormarton

Start	Home Farm in Hawkesbury Upton
Finish	Road junction in centre of Tormarton
Distance	12.1km (7½ miles)
Ascent	260m
Descent	285m
Time	3hr 30min
Refreshments	Old Sodbury
Accommodation	Little Sodbury, Old Sodbury and Tormarton

After Wotton-under-Edge – and certainly after Hawkesbury Upton – the CW levels out, with fewer sharp climbs and drops, and less woodland. The climbs are 100m rather than 200m and the views, while extensive, are more rolling. There is plenty of interest still, with the charming villages of Horton, Little Sodbury and Old Sodbury, more hill forts and a stroll across the extensive parkland of Dodington Park. This stage can easily be combined with Stage 11. There are scattered accommodation options beyond Tormarton, but many CW walkers choose to combine the final two stages after Tormarton and go all the way to Bath.

Hawkesbury Upton to Little Sodbury (5.5km, 1hr 30min)

Approaching from the Somerset Monument, turn right immediately after Home Farm and then bear left onto the track of the ancient Bath Lane, with hedgerows either side, shortly becoming open on the left. After 30min, follow the path as it stays in fields alongside Highfield Lane. Take a path bearing right to the top of a wood and, as you leave this, stay on a higher path through fields above **Horton Court** (rather than the Monarch's Way, which you have shared much of the trail with, and which takes a lower route here).

Horton Court is one of the oldest inhabited houses in England; parts still in use today were built in 1140, less than 80 years after the Normans arrived. The Norman Hall and a detached ambulatory (Italian-style loggia) are opened to the public by the National Trust on set days between April and October. The manor was originally occupied by a son of King Harold. The hall is all

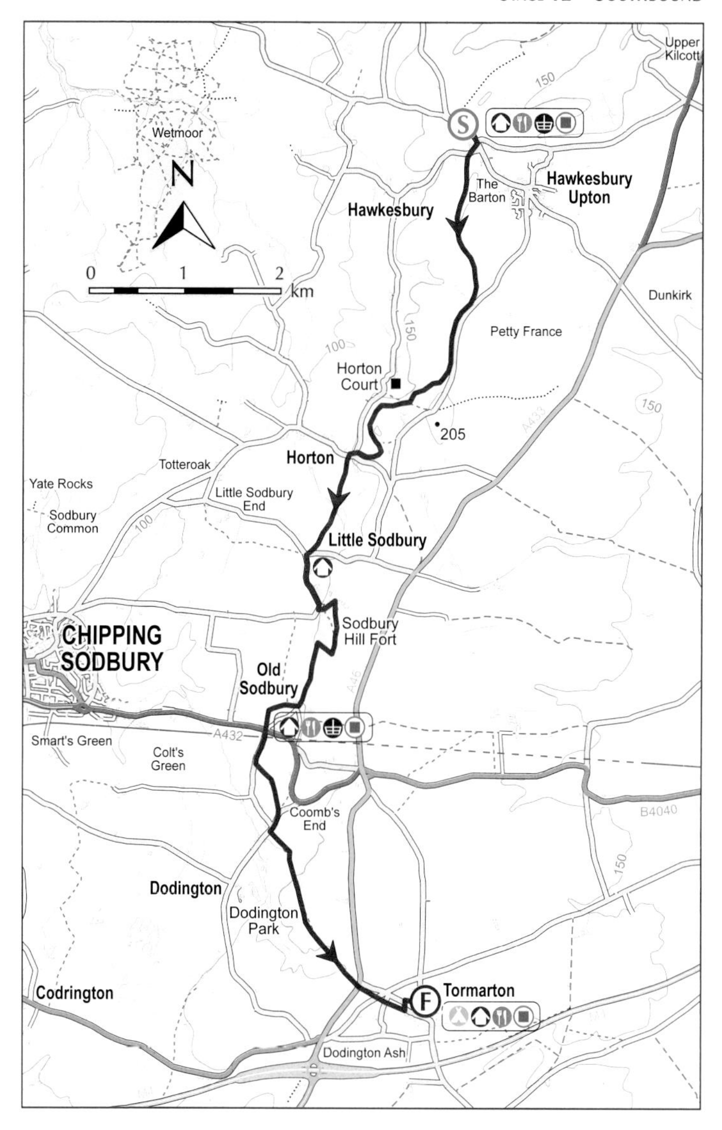
Upper Kilcott
150
Wetmoor
S
N
0 1 2 km
The Barton
Hawkesbury Upton
Hawkesbury
Dunkirk
Petty France
150
100
Horton Court
150
205
A433
Horton
Totteroak
Yate Rocks
Little Sodbury End
Sodbury Common
100
Little Sodbury
CHIPPING SODBURY
Sodbury Hill Fort
Old Sodbury
A46
A432
Smart's Green
Colt's Green
Coomb's End
B4040
150
Dodington
Dodington Park
Codrington
Tormarton
F
Dodington Ash

that remains of the original construction. Later additions inspired by Italian architecture were added in 1520 by William Knight, chief secretary to Henry VIII, and these now form the main part of the house.

Continue through fields, then left up a zig-zag path in a brief section of wood, passing through the site of a substantial hill fort. Turn right in the next field below a large house and pass an elegant folly (built as a millennium project to encourage nesting barn owls and swallows). The path veers right then left to enter the village of Horton near a large farm.

Turn right and then left and descend to pass a reservoir before coming to **Little Sodbury** near its church.

Little Sodbury is a tiny hamlet with a manor built in 1486 for Sir John Walsh. In 1521 William Tyndale came here as chaplain to Sir John's household. He began translating Erasmus's *Enchiridion Militis Christiani* into English and preaching in what was then seen to be an outspoken manner. The original Church of St Adeline, where he preached, was demolished in 1859 and its stone was used to build the current church, which can be seen here today.

Little Sodbury to Old Sodbury (2.8km, 50min)

Turn left by the church in Little Sodbury and take the quiet lane to pass Little Sodbury Manor. Just after the entrance, take a path across a field with fruit trees and climb through woods above the Manor. Turn right by houses and enter **Sodbury Hill Fort**, an 11-acre space.

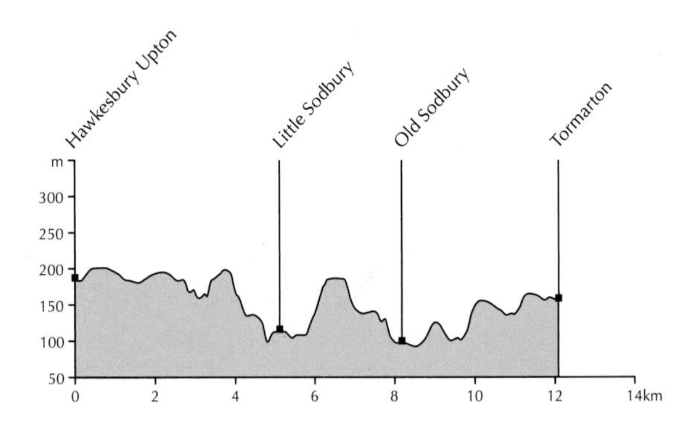

It's hard to get a good feel for the vast 11-acre hill fort at Little Sodbury

Sodbury Hill Fort is one of the most impressive on the walk. Covering 11 acres (4.5 hectares) of land, it is enclosed by a double set of ramparts and ditches. Constructed in the Iron Age, but considerably strengthened by the Romans, it is thought to have been used as a frontier post. Although it has never been excavated, a few Roman coins have been found in the turf. The Saxon army camped in the shelter of the ramparts in AD577, and in 1471 Edward IV rested here with his army on the way to do battle with Margaret of Anjou at Tewkesbury during the Wars of the Roses for the English crown.

After the fort, turn right and then left and follow the path, passing the school, then keep right through **Old Sodbury** churchyard. Drop down through a field and cross another field past farm buildings to reach a junction with the Dog Inn (accommodation, refreshments) opposite and a small shop at the petrol station to the right.

Old Sodbury to Tormarton (3.8km, 1hr 10min)
Continue ahead through the village past the Dog Inn. Two paths leave the road; take the second on the left, angled across fields. Turn right at a road and, in 200 metres, find the entrance to **Dodington Park** on the left, with signs warning of cameras and guards. The main house (not open to the public) is 500 metres further along the road.

Water features in Dodington Park

Dodington Park is a manicured park and estate, which is currently owned by a vacuum cleaner magnate. The signs for cameras and security guards are only slightly off-putting, since neither cameras nor guards are visible, and the Grade II-listed park retains the charms that landscaper Capability Brown imbued in it in the 1760s.

Keeping to the path, follow a line of trees and then veer right along a walkway between fields. Cross the infant River Frome by a bridge and climb to the fast and busy A46 road.

Cross the road and fields. Cross the B4465 road, then cross another road and follow the path through fields to the church and the junction in the centre of the village, near the former Major's Retreat pub.

Accommodation in **Tormarton** is at the Compass Inn (hotel allows camping) on the B4465 road, which was crossed on the route entering the village. There is no footpath so take care walking along the roadside.

NORTHBOUND FROM TORMARTON TO HAWKESBURY UPTON (12.1km, 3hr 20min)

This stage passes through the sweeping parkland surrounding Dodington Park, then visits the villages of Old Sodbury and Little Sodbury, between which a huge hill fort is situated on the escarpment edge. After Little Sodbury the CW rises again passing above Horton Court then along an ancient lane past vast fields to reach Hawkesbury Upton.

Tormarton to Old Sodbury (3.8km, 1hr)

From the centre of the village, walk up to visit the church then follow signs over a series of walls between small fields to cross the B4465. Continue directly over another field to cross the A46 then over a stile into **Dodington Park**. Posts direct you down to a footbridge over the infant River Frome, then over more meadows and down to a stone bridge with a more ornate water feature seen to the left. Veer left and leave the Park onto a road and turn right uphill for about 200 metres. Take a path to the left across two fields now heading down to meet a road where you turn right and walk into the village of **Old Sodbury**, with the Dog Inn (accommodation, refreshments) on the right at a crossroads and a shop opposite.

Old Sodbury to Little Sodbury (2.8km, 50min)

Cross directly over the crossroads and through a farm, then diagonally right up two fields heading towards the church. Pass through the churchyard then left up a narrow lane beside the school. This leads to a path at the top right of a long field by a wood. At the end of this field, turn sharply right and climb steeply onto the escarpment and the impressive Sodbury Hill Fort. Cross the hill fort then go sharply left down through woods to a narrow lane. Turn right down to the hamlet of **Little Sodbury**, with a church at its centre.

Little Sodbury to Hawkesbury Upton (5.5km, 1hr 30min)

Turn right at the church, then turn immediately left across a series of fields, past a small reservoir on the right then up to the village of **Horton**. Turn right then immediately left on a road, then turn immediately left again onto a rising path across a sloping field with a large house ahead and a stone folly on the left. Exit the field at the top left and continue on the escarpment before dropping again through a strip of steep woodland, then go right to climb yet again through woods then across rough fields. These lead to a broad track hugging the left edge of vast fields and reaching the edge of **Hawkesbury Upton** at a road junction and triangle duck pond. The village is mainly to the right up the hill.

STAGE 13

Tormarton to Cold Ashton

Start	Junction in centre of Tormarton
Finish	Church in Cold Ashton
Distance	10.4km (6½ miles)
Ascent	240m
Descent	205m
Time	3hr
Refreshments	Pennsylvania
Accommodation	Pennsylvania and Cold Ashton

This is a short stage, with accommodation options at or near Cold Ashton. The stage is characterised by paths crossing fields, which mainly stay high, but which also make numerous road crossings – some of busy roads, which require care. The ancient deer park at Dyrham, and its elegant and imposing house, is a highlight. Since this stage is very short, it is often combined with Stage 14 to walk directly to Bath. There is an additional accommodation option on Stage 14 at Lansdown (off-route), should you wish to break up the final stage.

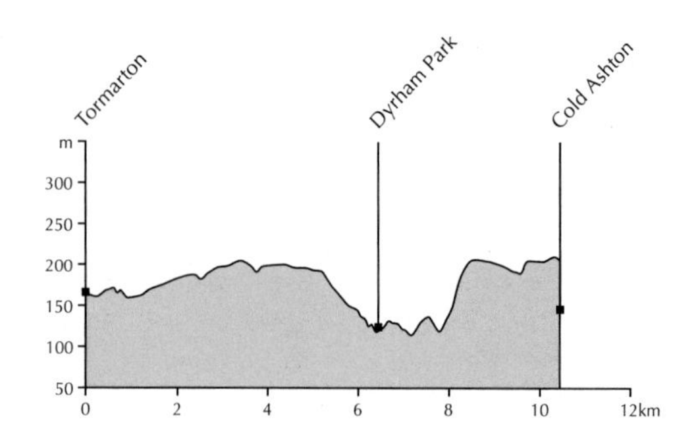

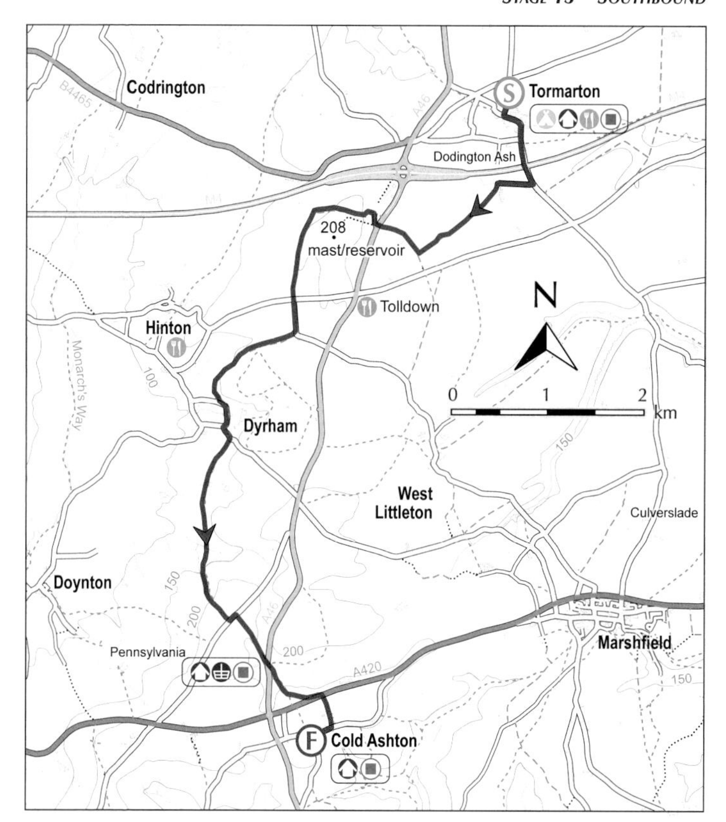

Tormarton to Dyrham Park (6.4km, 1hr 45min)

From the road junction in the centre of Tormarton, head left out of the village. Follow the road as it crosses the M4 and turn right on a minor road to Lower Lapdown Farm. Pass through, leaving the farm buildings to your left, then pass a house and continue alongside fields.

Turn right at the end of a field (at the last inspection the sign incorrectly pointed left). Follow the path through an area of bushes, likely to be overgrown, and reach the A46 again. A formal crossing with no crossing lights is slightly left. Head right on an access road into a wood, Beacon Lane Plantation, and follow the myriad tracks to the end of this and a mast by signs to an underground reservoir. Continue into fields and follow the path as it bears left, soon coming to a minor road. Pubs for refreshments are 1km east at the Crown near Tolldown Farm (also accommodation) and west at the Bull pub in Hinton.

Cross the road and continue along another road – Field Lane. Turn right into fields as the road bears left and follow the path around the edge of the deer park, coming out onto a road near the impressive view of **Dyrham Park House**.

DYRHAM PARK

Dyrham Park is an ancient deer park covering 274 acres (111 hectares) of grassland, and the herd of fallow deer is reckoned to be one of the oldest in the country. Dyrham comes from the Anglo-Saxon word 'dirham', meaning deer enclosure, first mentioned in a document of AD577. The grounds, which surround the imposing Dyrham House, are formerly terraced and landscaped with water gardens, featuring a great waterspout and a cascade pouring over a series of more than 200 steps.

The present house was built for William Blathwayt and is actually two houses standing back to back to replace an original Tudor mansion, although there are records from 1086 of a Manor at Dyrham recorded in the Domesday Book. The older of the houses was built at the end of the 17th century, the other about six years later (finished around 1704). Now in the care of the National Trust, the house is open daily from 11:30–16:00 (limited hours during the winter), while the park is open throughout the year.

Dyrham House

Looking across fields to Pennsylvania

Dyrham Park to Cold Ashton (4.0km, 1hr 15min)

From Dyrham, continue and turn left on a road that climbs a little before turning right onto a path through fields. Continue cross-country for 20min and climb the path through Dyrham Wood. Cross a field to a busy B-road and turn left, then after 100 metres turn right. Continue alongside fields to reach **Pennsylvania**, a hamlet with B&B accommodation and a shop attached to the petrol station soon after.

Cross the fast A46 road and head out across fields coming to the A420. Keep left for 75 metres and turn right along a driveway, pass a large house and enter the churchyard of the Holy Trinity Church to reach Hyde's Lane in **Cold Ashton**.

> **Cold Ashton** is so named as it catches the full force of winds that sweep in off the Bristol Channel. There are fine views that overlook land on which medieval farmers grew vines. The gabled Elizabethan manor, with its tall chimneys and ornate gateway, stands next door to the rectory, but remains partially hidden from the Cotswold Way route. It was in Cold Ashton Manor that Sir Bevil Grenville died on the night of 5 July 1643 following the Battle of Lansdown in the Civil War – his memorial is passed on the final stage.

NORTHBOUND FROM COLD ASHTON TO TORMARTON (10.4km, 2hr 45min)

Although punctuated by numerous road crossings, this stage crosses rolling fields and pastures, then goes through the hamlet of Dyrham, with Dyrham Park and its associated deer park seen on the right.

Cold Ashton to Dyrham Park (4.0km, 1hr 5min)
Walk through the village admiring the views to the right, then take the path on the left through the churchyard of the Holy Trinity Church and continue ahead to the A420. Cross over and head left then diagonally across fields to reach the A46. Cross this road and, maintaining direction, continue across more fields to reach an equally busy B-road. Turn left then shortly right into more fields, heading for Dyrham Wood. Descend through the wood, cross a stream and continue, now directly north, undulating over the lower scarp slopes, then down into **Dyrham**, with Dyrham Park on the right.

Dyrham Park to Tormarton (6.4km, 1hr 40min)
After passing in front of Dyrham Park, turn right onto a path and follow this around the edge of the deer park, climbing steadily to reach Field Lane. Turn left along the lane then cross straight over a road and continue across the edge of a series of fields with a mast seen ahead to the right. The path bears right, past the mast and a reservoir then along the edge of Beacon Lane Plantation to a service road. Turn right, then cross the A46 onto a track which curves right, rising slightly to a junction of paths. Turn left and, keeping to the edge of a series of large fields, pass to the left of Lower Lapdown Farm buildings leading onto a lane, then turn left to cross over the M4 motorway and walk into the village of **Tormarton**.

STAGE 14

Cold Ashton to Bath

Start	Church in Cold Ashton
Finish	Bath Abbey
Distance	16.7km (10½ miles)
Ascent	370m
Descent	540m
Time	4hr 30min
Refreshments	None until Bath
Accommodation	Lansdown village (1km off-route) and Bath

This last stage does not disappoint in any way. It visits the site of the 1643 Battle of Lansdown, then takes a rather convoluted circuit of a golf course, with views and one last hill fort. Bath Racecourse leads to Prospect Stile, providing the first views down to Bath, then the route heads down to the suburb of Weston. One final, possibly unwelcome, climb to Primrose Hill avoids urban roads and traffic before a descent to pass Bath's highlights: the Royal Crescent, the Circus, the Roman Baths, the Pump Room and glorious Bath Abbey.

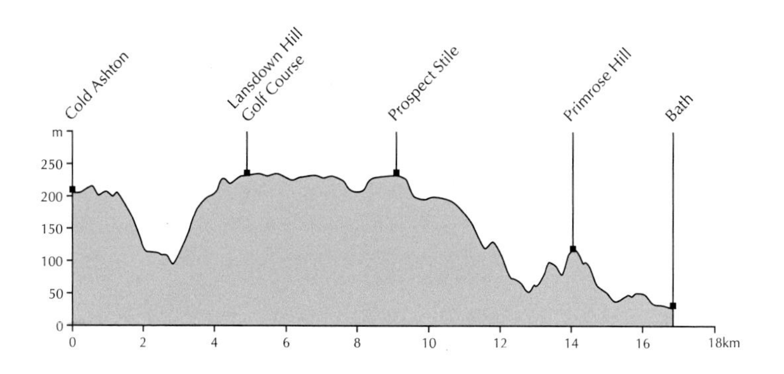

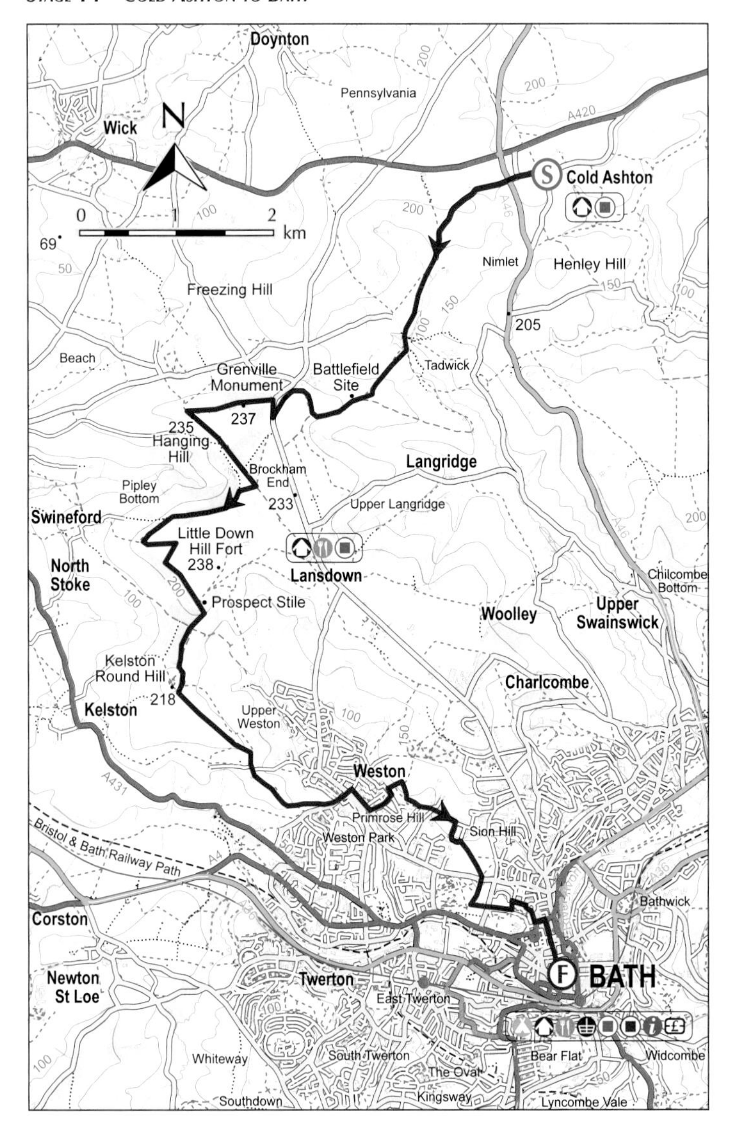
Doynton
Pennsylvania
Wick
N
0
1
2
km
69
50
100
200
A420
Cold Ashton
A46
Nimlet
Henley Hill
150
205
Freezing Hill
Beach
Grenville Monument
Battlefield Site
Tadwick
237
235
Hanging Hill
Brockham End
233
Langridge
Upper Langridge
Pipley Bottom
Swineford
Little Down Hill Fort
238
Lansdown
North Stoke
Prospect Stile
Chilcombe Bottom
Upper Swainswick
Woolley
Kelston Round Hill
218
Kelston
Charlcombe
Upper Weston
Weston
A431
Primrose Hill
Sion Hill
Weston Park
Bristol & Bath Railway Path
A4
A36
Bathwick
Corston
BATH
Newton St Loe
Twerton
East Twerton
Whiteway
South Twerton
The Oval
Bear Flat
Widcombe
Southdown
Kingsway
Lyncombe Vale

Cold Ashton to Lansdown Hill (4.7km, 1hr 20min)

Turn right by the church and walk through the village down a minor road. Cross the A46 (for the final time on the walk). Follow the Greenway Lane down past the Hill Farm nursery, then ahead over a stream where the track bends left. Take the path nearest the reservoir to reach farm buildings and houses, then turn left, go over a cattle grid, then go right and climb across two fields. After 75 metres join an enclosed lane, rising through fields, and emerge at a board explaining the **battle site**. Continue through the wall and follow the path round to the substantial **Grenville Monument**, soon coming to a road.

The **Grenville Monument** marks an area known as the Battlefields on Lansdown Hill, where, on 5 July 1643, Royalist troops pursued a Parliamentarian army led by Sir William Waller into what became remembered as the Battle of Lansdown. During the pursuit up the hill, Waller's men fired their cannon into the Royalists, but Sir Bevil Grenville stormed the hill on horseback in an attempt to stop the guns. He was successful, causing the Parliamentarians to retreat, but at the moment his Cornishmen broke through, Grenville was hit and mortally wounded. He was carried to Cold Ashton Manor, where he died the same night. Of some 2000 Royalists taking part in the battle, only 600 are thought to have survived. The monument was erected in 1720 by Sir Bevil's grandson, Lord Lansdown.

Lansdown Hill to Prospect Stile (4.5km, 1hr 10min)

Cross the road and find an access lane to the right just beyond it. Take this lane and continue on the track alongside the lane. Pass a radio mast, bear left and continue into fields, coming to the trig point at **Hanging Hill**.

Turn left and continue along the field side. Pass a wall and join a track coming into the golf course. Turn right and keep on the track between a wood and a fairway, and at the end of the wood turn right on a sparsely signed path across the course. (For accommodation at the Charlcombe Inn at Lansdown, continue ahead past the golf clubhouse.) Join a track alongside Pipley Wood, leave the course through a gate and, after 75 metres, find a track branching left (the map here marks the CW route somewhat above the track – wrongly there is no route there). Under a steep embankment, find a left turn and climb to the earthwork and fort.

The most westerly point on the Cotswold Way, **Little Down Hill Fort** is an Iron Age site of about 15 acres (6 hectares) with a rampart and single ditch which can still be easily identified.

The view from Prospect Stile over Bath

Keep right after the fort and follow field edges, passing through the grounds of Bath Racecourse. Come to **Prospect Stile**, with wide-ranging views over the descending route, with Kelston Round Hill ahead, and Weston and Bath far below.

Prospect Stile to Bath (7.5km, 2hr)

Having taken in the view, drop down from Prospect Stile on waymarked paths alongside fields. Pass under the elegant hilltop of **Kelston Round Hill** and continue to descend. Cross a road by Pendean Farm and continue through fields, then descend past playing fields to come to a road that descends into **Weston**.

Now it gets fiddly. For the final part of the stage, you will take a detour up Primrose Hill and then descend almost directly into the centre of Bath – there are, however, a lot of twists and turns. The route to the centre of Bath is sparsely signed. (Other routes through Bath can be taken.)

Take a quieter road forking left and come to a road crossing. Cross and then continue right on High Street (the slightly higher of the two parallel roads) towards All Saints Church. Take the next road left (Church Road). Climb straight up to a small water treatment works to come out on Primrose Hill. Turn right and follow the path across the common, then along several narrow and surprisingly steep paths among the houses of **Sion Hill**, before turning abruptly right (the signpost isabout 4m above your head) and starting to drop down.

Enter the open space of the High Common (a sometime golf course too) and recross Weston Road. Follow the road left and pass the park nursery onto Royal Avenue and the Victoria Monument.

Now it gets even fiddlier through the streets of central **Bath**. Take the next left and then immediately head right on a walkway across the front of the famous Royal Crescent (built in the 18th century), one of the finest examples of Georgian architecture in Britain. After the Crescent, turn left and then right on Brock Street to enter the Circus, an elegant circle of Georgian buildings.

Turn right from the Circus down Gay Street to Queen Square. Turn left at the end of the square on Wood Street, then right onto Milsom Street and continue ahead through the narrow Burton Street that runs into Union Street, then Stall Street. Turn left under the stone arch to Abbey Yard, where you will find Bath Abbey, the Roman Baths, and the Pump Room. By the abbey, find the finish marker, a twin of the start marker in Chipping Campden.

You have reached the end of the trail – congratulations. Bath has all facilities and plenty of (expensive) hotels and restaurants. The Roman Baths are well worth a visit, as is the elegant abbey. It's a compact but busy city, and there is much to see.

Bath Abbey – the end of the Cotswold Way trail

BATH

Bath is the only UK city designated as a UNESCO World Heritage Site, and it has also been designated one of the Great Spa Towns of Europe by UNESCO. There is evidence that human activity around the hot springs dates from 8000BC; according to legend, Prince Bladud founded the city of Bath around the springs. Known by the Romans as Aquae Sulis (the waters of the sun), the hot springs are unique in the UK, and the baths were developed from AD43 as a complex for rest and relaxation. In AD70 a reservoir around the springs was built, followed by a series of baths and rooms of different temperatures, a gymnasium and a temple to the Goddess Sulis Minerva.

The spring water rises at a constant temperature of 120°F (50°C) at a flow of around 250,000 gallons (1,136,500 litres) per day. It is known for its healing properties, promising relief from rheumatism, gout, lumbago, sciatica and neuritis. After the Romans left England in around AD350, the Saxons rebuilt the town and founded an abbey. In AD973 Dunstan, Archbishop of Canterbury, crowned Edgar the first King of all England here.

Between 1688 and 1703, Bath became a fashionable resort after Queen Anne began 'taking the waters' and Beau Nash made Bath the social heart of the country, leading to the 18th-century layout and architecture still seen today. Among Bath's many famous residents was Jane Austin, who lived in the city for five years, and Bath became the setting for two of her works: *Northanger Abbey* and *Persuasion*.

Oliver King, the Bishop of Bath and Wells from 1495–1503, helped to rebuild the magnificent abbey seen today, resplendent with carvings and fan-vaulted ceilings. King Henry VII's royal masons, Robert and William Vertue, were employed to design the famous fan-vaulted ceiling to the east of the tower. After the dissolution of the monasteries, the abbey fell into ruin, then in 1573 Queen Elizabeth I licensed a seven-year nationwide collection to support the rebuilding of the abbey over the course of the following 50 years. The abbey replaces an even larger Norman cathedral, first constructed in 1090.

Today, Bath has more to offer than the reputation of its waters, although the modern Thermae Bath Spa provides superb facilities. Bath's heritage is of the Romans, and its spirit lies behind the glory of its abbey and the architectural genius of the Regency period.The modern tourist information centre at Abbey Chambers has countless leaflets, maps and guidebooks available, but for a preview of what's on and where in Bath, go to www.visitbath.co.uk or www.cotswolds.info/places/bath.

NORTHBOUND FROM BATH TO COLD ASHTON (16.7km, 4hr 40min)

You are about to embark on a trail which, right from the start, will take you to fine viewpoints, past ancient hill forts and through stone villages – the very essence of the Cotswold Way. To begin with, there is a convoluted route out of Bath to negotiate before climbing to the first viewpoint, then the route continues to a hill fort and more fine views. Cross Civil War battlefields, then head on across rolling fields to Cold Ashton, the first of many attractive villages.

Bath to Prospect Stile (7.5km, 2hr 10min)

With your back to Bath Abbey, walk under the arch and turn right into Stall Street, then continue ahead into Union Street and Burton Street, then left onto Quiet Street, which leads into Wood Street to reach Queen Square. Turn right and head up Gay Street into the Royal Circus and keep left into Brock Street. At the end of Brock Street turn left then right on paths across the grass which lead past the impressive Royal Crescent.

Pulteney Bridge over the River Avon in Bath

The Grenville Monument on Lansdown Hill

Turn left then immediately right onto Royal Avenue, past the Victoria Obelisk, then curve right and head up the right side of parkland. Cross straight over Weston Road onto an enclosed path heading uphill. Turn right up **Sion Hill**, then turn left at the top, following CW signs along Summerhill Road, then continue along a series of steep enclosed paths, keeping just above houses. Turn left at a water treatment works and now drop directly downhill. Turn right just beyond All Saints Church and follow Church Street then High Street to a road junction. Cross with care and turn left then immediately right up Anchor Road for 150 metres, then take a path signed right across playing fields. Here, climb more steeply onto Dean Hill and witness your first views back to Weston and Bath.

Keep to the top side of the field and drop to Pendean Farm, then continue straight ahead up a rough track leading onto a path, passing just to the right of **Kelston Round Hill**, and continue on this path with a final, briefly steeper, climb to **Prospect Stile**, with fine views. (For accommodation at the Charlcombe Inn, turn right then branch right again to the village of Lansdown.)

Prospect Stile to Lansdown Hill (4.5km, 1hr 10min)

Keep to the left margin, passing the edge of Bath Racecourse then along the low ramparts of a hill fort, then turn left to cross the hill fort. Drop steeply and turn sharp right on a track over fields then bear right, rising to a gate onto a golf course. Keep to the track between Pipley Wood and the golf course, then bear right by a building to cross a fairway. Turn left, now with the fairway on your left, and at the end bear left to follow a wall to a trig point at **Hanging Hill**.

Turn right along the scarp edge then join a path beside a service road. Shortly after the service road turns sharply right, pass through a gap and cross directly over the main road to reach information boards marking the site of the Battle of Lansdown (1643). Follow the path to the **Grenville Monument**, then continue through light woodland and around the left side of the grassy **battlefield** to a stone stile.

Lansdown Hill to Cold Ashton (4.7km, 1hr 20min)

Turn left and follow a grassy track which becomes more enclosed, then leave the track through a gap in the hedge at the corner of a field. Go through a gate then descend diagonally across two large fields to a track, turn left over a cattle grid then right just past farm buildings into fields.

Follow the path across fields to reach a stream and join a track, rising past Hill Farm nurseries, and continue uphill, passing through more farm buildings to reach the A46. Cross straight over and up into the village of **Cold Ashton** on Hyde's Lane.

APPENDIX A

Useful contacts

The Cotswold Way National Trail
www.nationaltrail.co.uk/cotswold-way

Cotswold Way Association
www.cotswoldwayassociation.org.uk

Explore the Cotswolds
www.explorethecotswolds.com

Cotswolds AONB
www.cotswoldsaonb.org.uk

Cotswolds Tourism Partnership
www.cotswolds.com

The Ramblers
www.ramblers.org.uk

Tourist information offices

Bath

Beau Nash House (next to Roman Baths)
www.visitbath.co.uk
https://bathvisitorinformation.co.uk

Broadway

Unit 14, Russell Square
Worcestershire WR12 7AP
tel 01386 852937
www.cotswolds.info/places/broadway
www.visit-broadway.co.uk
www.broadway-cotswolds.co.uk

Cheltenham

www.visitcheltenham.com

Chipping Campden

The Old Police Station
High Street, Gloucestershire GL55 6HB
tel 01386 841206
www.chippingcampden.co.uk
www.cotswolds.info/places/chipping-campden
www.chippingcampdenonline.org

Stroud

www.cotswolds.info/places/stroud

Winchcombe

The Town Hall
High Street, Gloucestershire GL54 5LJ
tel 01242 602925
www.cotswolds.info/places/winchcombe
www.winchcombe.co.uk

Painswick

St Mary's Church
tel 01452 812278
painswicktouristinfo.co.uk

Wootton-under-Edge

The Heritage Centre
The Chipping, Wotton-under-Edge
Gloucestershire GL12 7AD
tel 01453 521541
www.wottonheritage.com
www.cotswolds.info/places/wotton-under-edge

Baggage transfer companies

Cotswold Luggage Transfers
tel 01386 840688
info@thevolunteerinn.net
www.luggage-transfers.co.uk

Carry-a-bag (baggage transfer & accommodation booking service)
tel 01242 250642
info@carryabag.co.uk
www.carryabag.co.uk

Sherpa Van (self-guided walking packages and baggage transfer)
tel 01748 826917
info@sherpavan.com

APPENDIX B

Accommodation along the route

This selection of available accommodation is arranged roughly in the order it appears to a walker heading southbound, from Chipping Campden to Bath. Hotels, guest houses, B&Bs and hostels are included. Self-catering is not included, as most require stays of two or more nights. All accommodation listed is within 1.5km of the route. Note: the Cotswold Way National Trail website contains a good accommodation list, although some listings are further from the route than would be ideal. See www.nationaltrail.co.uk/cotswold-way.

Chipping Campden

Frances Cottage
Lower High Street
(2 rooms)
tel 01386 840894
jill.j.slade@btopenworld.com

Bantam Tea Rooms and B&B
High Street
(8 rooms)
tel 01386 840386

The Red Lion Inn
Lower High Street
(4 rooms)
tel 01386 840760
info@redliontavern.co.uk

Stonecroft B&B
George Lane
(2 rooms)
tel 01386 840486
info@stonecroft-chippingcampden.co.uk

Taplins
5 Aston Road
(3 rooms)
tel 01386 840927
info@cotswoldwaystay.co.uk

The Chance
1 Aston Road
(4 rooms)
tel 01386 849079
enquiries@the-chance.co.uk

The Old Bakehouse
Lower High Street
(2 rooms)
tel 01386 840979
zoegabb@yahoo.co.uk

The Volunteer Inn
Lower High Street
(9 rooms)
tel 01386 840688
info@thevolunteerinn.net

Broadway

Brook House Guest House
Station Road
(5 rooms)
tel 01386 852313
brookhousebb@googlemail.com

Cowley House
Church Street
(8 rooms)
tel 01386 858148
joan.peter@cowleyhouse-broadway.co.uk

The Crown and Trumpet
Church Street
(5 rooms)
tel 01386 853202
crownandtrumpetinn@gmail.com

The Horse and Hound
54 High Street
tel 01386 852287

The Lodge
2 Kiel Close
High Street
(9 rooms)
tel 01386 852007
info@thelodgebroadway.co.uk

Old Station House
Station Road
(4 rooms)
tel 01386 852659
oldstationhousecotswolds@gmail.com

Small Talk Lodge
32 High Street
(4 rooms)
tel 01386 858953
bookings@smalltalklodge.co.uk

Windrush House
Station Road
(5 rooms)
tel 01386 853577
info@windrushhouse.com

Stanton
The Old Post House
(2 rooms)
tel 01386 584398
jo.imeson1@gmail.com

Shenberrow Hill
(3 rooms)
tel 01386 584468
michael.neilan1@btopenworld.com

Stanton Guildhouse
(8 rooms)
tel 07784 240166
info@stantonguildhouse.org.uk

The Vine
(3 rooms)
tel 01386 584250
info@cotswoldsriding.co.uk

Wood Stanway
Wood Stanway Farmhouse
(3 rooms)
tel 01386 584318
greensbedandbreakfast@gmail.com

Nr Beckbury Camp
North Farmcote Farm B&B
(3 rooms)
tel 01242 602304
davideayrs@yahoo.co.uk

Winchcombe
Blair House
41 Gretton Road
(3 rooms)
tel 01242 603626
info@blairhousewinchcombe.co.uk

One Silk Mill Lane
(2 rooms)
tel 01242 603952
jenny.cheshire@virgin.net

The Lion Inn
37 North Street
(9 rooms)
tel 01242 603300
thelioninnwinchcombe@butcombepubs.
com

The Plaisterers Arms
Abbey Terrace
(5 rooms)
tel 01242 602358
plaisterers.arms@btinternet.com

The White Hart Inn
High Street
(11 rooms)
tel 01242 602359
info@whitehartwinchcombe.co.uk

Wesley House
High Street
(5 rooms)
tel 01242 602366
enquiries@wesleyhouse.co.uk

Cleeve Common
Postlip Hall Farm
tel 01242 603351
valerie-albutt@btconnect.com

Cleeve Hill
The Rising Sun Hotel
(23 rooms)
tel 01242 676281

Gambles Farm
Gambles Lane
Woodmancote
(2 rooms)
tel 01242 677719
gamblesfarm@mail.com

Cleeve Hill Hotel
(12 rooms)
tel 01242 672052
post@cleevehillhotel.co.uk

Malvern View Hotel
(7 rooms)
tel 01242 672017
info@malvernview.com

Dowdeswell/Charlton Kings
The Charlton Boutique Hotel
London Road
(13 rooms)
tel 01242 651051
enquiries@thecharlton.co.uk

Birdlip

The Royal George Hotel
(34 rooms)
tel 01452 862506

Painswick
Hambutts Mynd
Edge Road
(3 rooms)
tel 01452 812352

Falcon Inn
New Street
(11 rooms)
tel 01452 222820

Orchard House
4 Court Orchard
(2 rooms)
tel 01452 813150
harleydy@btinternet.com

St Annes B&B
Gloucester Road
(3 rooms)
tel 01452 812879
iris@st-annes-painswick.co.uk

St Michael's House
Victoria Street
(5 rooms)
tel 01452 812712
hello@stmichaelsbistro.co.uk

Tibbiwell Lodge
Tibbiwell Lane
(3 rooms)
tel 01452 812748
lovell_richard@hotmail.com

Troy House
Gloucester Street
(3 rooms)
tel 01452 812339
troyhouse@outlook.com

King's Stanley
Orchardene
Castle Street
(2 rooms)
tel 01453 822684
info@orchardene.co.uk

The Grey Cottage
Bath Road
Leonard Stanley
(3 rooms)
tel 01453 822515
rosemary.reeves@btinternet.com

Middleyard
Valley Views
12 Orchard Close
(3 rooms)
tel 01453 827458
enquiries@valley-views.com

Greencourt Loft
Greencourt House
Stonehouse
tel 07967 153813

Selsley
The Bell Inn
Bell Lane
tel 01453 753801
info@thebellinnselsley.com

Dursley
Foresters
31 Chapel Street
(3 rooms)
tel 01453 549996
foresters@freeuk.com

Ye Olde Dursley Hotel
Long Street
tel 01453 542821

Underhill House
4 Hill Road
(2 rooms)
tel 01453 549617

Woodland House
(6 rooms)
tel 01453 298773
woodlandhousebnb@gmail.com

North Nibley
Forthay B&B
Forthay, just north of North Nibley
(3 rooms)
tel 01453 549016
forthaybandb@gmail.com

The Black Horse Inn
(6 rooms)
tel 01453 453895
d.yateshospitality@outlook.com

Wotton-under-Edge
The Swan Hotel
16 Market Street
tel 01453 843004
info@swanhotelwotton.com

Hawkesbury Upton
Bodkin House Hotel
Petty France
tel 01454 238310
info@thebodkin.co.uk

Little Sodbury
Cottage Courtyard
Totteroak Farm
Self catering
tel 07990 573749
ellewilliams@live.co.uk

Daisy Cottage
Crosslands Farm
tel 07770 680094

Old Sodbury
Hammerdown B&B
(2 rooms)
tel 01454 323776

Cross Hands Hotel
(21 rooms)
tel 01454 313000

Rock Cottage
The Hill
tel 01454 314688

The Dog Inn
(4 rooms)
tel 01454 312006
thedoginnoldsodbury@gmail.com

The Bell
Badminton Road
(4 rooms)
tel 01454 325582
info@thebellatoldsodbury.co.uk

Sodbury House Hotel
(7 rooms)
tel 01454 312847
info@sodburyhouse.co.uk

Tormarton
The Compass Inn
tel 0844 387 6056
www.bestwestern.co.uk

The Crown Inn
Tolldown
Dyrham
(9 rooms)
tel 01225 8911166
crowntolldown@butcombepubs.com

Noades House
(3 rooms)
tel 01454 218278
hi@noadesstudio.co.uk

Old Hundred Coach House
(1 room)
tel 01454 218420
deedaveb@yahoo.co.uk

Pennsylvania
Swan Cottage
4 rooms
tel 01225 891419
https://swancottagebandb.co.uk

Cold Ashton
Hill Farm
1 mile (1½km) out of the village on Stage 13
(2 rooms)
tel 01225 891952

Toghill House Farm
Freezing Hill
1.5 miles west of Cold Ashton
(5 rooms plus 2 glamping self-catering pitches)
tel 01225 891261
reservation@toghillhousefarm.co.uk

Lansdown (1km off-route)
Charlcombe Inn
(10 rooms)
tel 01225 421995
bookings@charlecombe.co.uk

Bath
YHA Bath
Bathwick Hill
(121 places)
tel 0845 371 9303
bath@yha.org.uk

Bath YMCA
Broad Street Place
(200 places)
tel 01225 325900
stay@ymca.bg.org

St Christopher's Inn
9 Green Street
(56 places)
tel 01225 481444

Devonshire House
143 Wellsway
(4 rooms)
tel 01225 312495
enquiries@devonshire-house.uk.com

Marlborough House
1 Marlborough Lane
(6 rooms)
tel 01225 318175
marlboroughguesthousebath.com

The Belmont B&B
7 Belmont
(4 rooms)
Lansdown Road
tel 01225 423082
stay@belmontbath.co.uk

Brooks Guest House
1 Crescent Gardens
(22 rooms)
tel 01225 425543
info@brooksguesthouse.com

Camping

Broadway
Northwick Farm
tel 07787 226010
northwickfarm@gmail.com

Hayles – Winchcombe
Hayles Fruit Farm
tel 01242 602123
info@haylesfruitfarm.co.uk

Dowdeswell
Colgate Farm Camping
www.colgatefarm.co.uk

Seven Springs
Big Skies Glamping and Camping
tel 07866 672831
www.bigskiesglamping.co.uk

Cooper's Hill
Buckshead Farm Campsite
B4070, 2km south of Birdlip
tel 017340 344979

Painswick
Painswick Glamping
(just west of Painswick)
Beech FarmBeech Lane
(5 pitches and pods)
tel 07866 520 636
info@painswickglamping.co.uk

Nympsfield
Woodleigh
(August only)
(30 basic pitches)
www.pitchup.com

North Nibley
Hunts Court Huts
(4 pitches and 2 glamping pods)
tel 01453 544632
contact@huntscourthuts.co.uk

Tormarton
Compass Inn
(Camping in field adjacent to hotel by arrangement)
tel 01454 218242

Bath
Blackberries Camping Park
Monkton Farleigh
tel 07791 562580
info@theblackberries.co.uk

APPENDIX C

Further reading

Bingham, Jane *The Cotswolds: A Cultural History* (Signal Books, 2015)

Brill, Edith *Life and Tradition on the Cotswolds* (Amberley, 2009)

Campbell, Sean *Hill-Forts of the Cotswolds* (Amberley Publishing, 2016)

Crosher, GR *Along the Cotswold Ways* (Littlehampton Book Services, 1976)

Gjika, Aleks *Gloucestershire in Photographs* (Amberley Publishing, 2018)

Hall, Damian *Walking in the Cotswolds* (Cicerone, 2021)

Hill, S *Spirit of the Cotswolds* (Michael Joseph, 1988)

Pilbeam, Alan *The Old Paths of Gloucestershire* (History Press, 2008)

Titmarsh, Peter *The Cotswold Town & Village Guide* (Reardon Publishing, 2000)

Verey, D *The Buildings of England: Gloucestershire 1 – The Cotswolds* (Pevsner Architectural Guides) (Yale University Press, 1999)

Ward, Greg *Pocket Oxford and the Cotswolds* (Lonely Planet, 2019)

Wright, L and Priddey, D *Cotswold Heritage* (Hale, 1977)

NOTES

NOTES

NOTES

NOTES

The summit of Cleeve Hill – the highest point on the trail

DOWNLOAD THE GPX FILES

All the routes in this guide are available for download from:

www.cicerone.co.uk/1210/GPX

as standard format GPX files. You should be able to load them into most online GPX systems and mobile devices, whether GPS or smartphone. You may need to convert the file into your preferred format using a conversion programme such as gpsvisualizer.com or one of the many other such websites and programmes.

When you follow this link, you will be asked for your email address and where you purchased the guidebook, and have the option to subscribe to the Cicerone e-newsletter.

www.cicerone.co.uk

LISTING OF CICERONE GUIDES

BRITISH ISLES CHALLENGES, COLLECTIONS AND ACTIVITIES

Cycling Land's End to John o' Groats
Great Walks on the England Coast Path
The Big Rounds
The Book of the Bivvy
The Book of the Bothy
The Mountains of England & Wales: Vol 1 Wales
Vol 2 England
The National Trails
Walking the End to End Trail

SHORT WALKS SERIES

Short Walks Hadrian's Wall
Short Walks in Arnside and Silverdale
Short Walks in Dumfries and Galloway
Short Walks in Nidderdale
Short Walks in the Lake District: Windermere Ambleside and Grasmere
Short Walks in the Surrey Hills
Short Walks Lake District – Coniston and Langdale
Short Walks on the Malvern Hills
Short Walks Winchester

SCOTLAND

Ben Nevis and Glen Coe
Cycle Touring in Northern Scotland
Cycling in the Hebrides
Cycling the North Coast 500
Great Mountain Days in Scotland
Mountain Biking in Southern and Central Scotland
Mountain Biking in West and North West Scotland
Not the West Highland Way Scotland
Scotland's Best Small Mountains
Scotland's Mountain Ridges
Scottish Wild Country Backpacking
Skye's Cuillin Ridge Traverse
The Borders Abbeys Way
The Great Glen Way
The Great Glen Way Map Booklet
The Hebridean Way
The Hebrides
The Isle of Mull
The Isle of Skye
The Skye Trail
The Southern Upland Way
The West Highland Way
The West Highland Way Map Booklet
Walking Ben Lawers, Rannoch and Atholl
Walking in the Cairngorms
Walking in the Pentland Hills
Walking in the Scottish Borders
Walking in the Southern Uplands
Walking in Torridon, Fisherfield, Fannichs and An Teallach
Walking Loch Lomond and the Trossachs
Walking on Arran
Walking on Harris and Lewis
Walking on Jura, Islay and Colonsay
Walking on Rum and the Small Isles
Walking on the Orkney and Shetland Isles
Walking on Uist and Barra
Walking the Cape Wrath Trail
Walking the Corbetts
Vol 1 South of the Great Glen
Vol 2 North of the Great Glen
Walking the Galloway Hills
Walking the John o' Groats Trail
Walking the Munros
Vol 1 – Southern, Central and Western Highlands
Vol 2 – Northern Highlands and the Cairngorms
Winter Climbs in the Cairngorms
Winter Climbs: Ben Nevis and Glen Coe

NORTHERN ENGLAND ROUTES

Cycling the Reivers Route
Cycling the Way of the Roses
Hadrian's Cycleway
Hadrian's Wall Path
Hadrian's Wall Path Map Booklet
The Coast to Coast Cycle Route
The Coast to Coast Walk
The Coast to Coast Walk Map Booklet
The Pennine Way
The Pennine Way Map Booklet
Walking the Dales Way
Walking the Dales Way Map Booklet

NORTH-EAST ENGLAND, YORKSHIRE DALES AND PENNINES

Cycling in the Yorkshire Dales
Great Mountain Days in the Pennines
Mountain Biking in the Yorkshire Dales
The Cleveland Way and the Yorkshire Wolds Way
The Cleveland Way Map Booklet
The North York Moors
Trail and Fell Running in the Yorkshire Dales
Walking in County Durham
Walking in Northumberland
Walking in the North Pennines
Walking in the Yorkshire Dales: North and East
Walking in the Yorkshire Dales: South and West
Walking St Cuthbert's Way
Walking St Oswald's Way and Northumberland Coast Path

NORTH-WEST ENGLAND AND THE ISLE OF MAN

Cycling the Pennine Bridleway
Isle of Man Coastal Path
The Lancashire Cycleway
The Lune Valley and Howgills
Walking in Cumbria's Eden Valley
Walking in Lancashire
Walking in the Forest of Bowland and Pendle
Walking on the Isle of Man
Walking on the West Pennine Moors
Walking the Ribble Way
Walks in Silverdale and Arnside

LAKE DISTRICT

Bikepacking in the Lake District
Cycling in the Lake District
Great Mountain Days in the Lake District
Joss Naylor's Lakes, Meres and Waters of the Lake District
Lake District Winter Climbs
Lake District: High Level and Fell Walks
Lake District: Low Level and Lake Walks
Mountain Biking in the Lake District
Outdoor Adventures with Children – Lake District
Scrambles in the Lake District – North
Scrambles in the Lake District – South
Trail and Fell Running in the Lake District
Walking The Cumbria Way
Walking the Lake District Fells:
Borrowdale
Buttermere
Coniston
Keswick
Langdale
Mardale and the Far East
Patterdale
Wasdale
Walking the Tour of the Lake District

DERBYSHIRE, PEAK DISTRICT AND MIDLANDS

Cycling in the Peak District
Dark Peak Walks
Scrambles in the Dark Peak
Walking in Derbyshire

Walking in the Peak District – White Peak East
Walking in the Peak District – White Peak West

SOUTHERN ENGLAND

20 Classic Sportive Rides:
In South East England
In South West England
Cycling in the Cotswolds
Mountain Biking on the North Downs
Mountain Biking on the South Downs
Suffolk Coast and Heath Walks
The Cotswold Way
The Cotswold Way Map Booklet
The Kennet and Avon Canal
The Lea Valley Walk
The North Downs Way
The North Downs Way Map Booklet
The Peddars Way and Norfolk Coast Path
The Pilgrims' Way
The Ridgeway National Trail
The Ridgeway National Trail Map Booklet
The South Downs Way
The South Downs Way Map Booklet
The Thames Path
The Thames Path Map Booklet
The Two Moors Way
Two Moors Way Map Booklet
Walking Hampshire's Test Way
Walking in Cornwall
Walking in Essex
Walking in Kent
Walking in London
Walking in Norfolk
Walking in the Chilterns
Walking in the Cotswolds
Walking in the Isles of Scilly
Walking in the New Forest
Walking in the North Wessex Downs
Walking on Dartmoor
Walking on Guernsey
Walking on Jersey
Walking on the Isle of Wight
Walking the Dartmoor Way
Walking the Jurassic Coast
Walking the South West Coast Path
Walking the South West Coast Path Map Booklets:
Vol 1: Minehead to St Ives
Vol 2: St Ives to Plymouth
Vol 3: Plymouth to Poole
Walks in the South Downs National Park

WALES AND WELSH BORDERS

Cycle Touring in Wales
Cycling Lon Las Cymru
Great Mountain Days in Snowdonia
Hillwalking in Shropshire
Mountain Walking in Snowdonia
Offa's Dyke Path
Offa's Dyke Path Map Booklet
Ridges of Snowdonia
Scrambles in Snowdonia
Snowdonia –
30 Low-level and Easy Walks:
– North
– South
The Cambrian Way
The Pembrokeshire Coast Path
The Snowdonia Way
The Wye Valley Walk
Walking in Carmarthenshire
Walking in Pembrokeshire
Walking in the Brecon Beacons
Walking in the Forest of Dean
Walking in the Wye Valley
Walking on Gower
Walking the Severn Way
Walking the Shropshire Way
Walking the Wales Coast Path

INTERNATIONAL CHALLENGES, COLLECTIONS AND ACTIVITIES

Europe's High Points
Walking the Via Francigena Pilgrim Route – Part 1

AFRICA

Kilimanjaro
Walking in the Drakensberg
Walks and Scrambles in the Moroccan Anti-Atlas

ALPS CROSS-BORDER ROUTES

100 Hut Walks in the Alps
Alpine Ski Mountaineering Vol 1 – Western Alps
The Karnischer Hohenweg
The Tour of the Bernina
Trail Running – Chamonix and the Mont Blanc region
Trekking Chamonix to Zermatt
Trekking in the Alps
Trekking in the Silvretta and Ratikon Alps
Trekking Munich to Venice
Trekking the Tour of Mont Blanc
Walking in the Alps

PYRENEES AND FRANCE/SPAIN CROSS-BORDER ROUTES

Shorter Treks in the Pyrenees
The GR11 Trail
The Pyrenean Haute Route
The Pyrenees
Walks and Climbs in the Pyrenees

AUSTRIA

Innsbruck Mountain Adventures
Trekking Austria's Adlerweg
Trekking in Austria's Hohe Tauern
Trekking in Austria's Zillertal Alps
Trekking in the Stubai Alps
Walking in Austria
Walking in the Salzkammergut: the Austrian Lake District

EASTERN EUROPE

The Danube Cycleway Vol 2
The Elbe Cycle Route
The High Tatras
The Mountains of Romania
Walking in Hungary

FRANCE, BELGIUM AND LUXEMBOURG

Camino de Santiago – Via Podiensis
Chamonix Mountain Adventures
Cycle Touring in France
Cycling London to Paris
Cycling the Canal de la Garonne
Cycling the Canal du Midi
Cycling the Route des Grandes Alpes
Mont Blanc Walks
Mountain Adventures in the Maurienne
Short Treks on Corsica
The GR5 Trail
The GR5 Trail – Benelux and Lorraine
The GR5 Trail – Vosges and Jura
The Grand Traverse of the Massif Central
The Moselle Cycle Route
The River Loire Cycle Route
The River Rhone Cycle Route
Trekking in the Vanoise
Trekking the Cathar Way
Trekking the GR10
Trekking the GR20 Corsica
Trekking the Robert Louis Stevenson Trail
Via Ferratas of the French Alps
Walking in Provence – East
Walking in Provence – West
Walking in the Ardennes
Walking in the Auvergne
Walking in the Brianconnais
Walking in the Dordogne
Walking in the Haute Savoie: North
Walking in the Haute Savoie: South
Walking on Corsica
Walking the Brittany Coast Path

GERMANY

Hiking and Cycling in the Black Forest
The Danube Cycleway Vol 1
The Rhine Cycle Route
The Westweg
Walking in the Bavarian Alps

IRELAND

The Wild Atlantic Way and Western Ireland
Walking the Wicklow Way

ITALY

Alta Via 1 / Alta Via 2 – Trekking in the Dolomites
Day Walks in the Dolomites
Italy's Grande Traversata delle Alpi
Italy's Sibillini National Park
Ski Touring and Snowshoeing in the Dolomites
The Way of St Francis
Trekking in the Apennines
Trekking the Giants' Trail: Alta Via 1 through the Italian Pennine Alps
Via Ferratas of the Italian Dolomites: Vols 1&2
Walking and Trekking in the Gran Paradiso
Walking in Abruzzo
Walking in Italy's Cinque Terre
Walking in Italy's Stelvio National Park
Walking in Sicily
Walking in the Aosta Valley
Walking in the Dolomites
Walking in Tuscany
Walking in Umbria
Walking Lake Como and Maggiore
Walking Lake Garda and Iseo
Walking on the Amalfi Coast
Walking the Via Francigena Pilgrim Route Parts 2 and 3
Walks and Treks in the Maritime Alps

MEDITERRANEAN

The High Mountains of Crete
Trekking in Greece
Walking and Trekking in Zagori
Walking and Trekking on Corfu
Walking in Cyprus
Walking on Malta
Walking on the Greek Islands – the Cyclades

NEW ZEALAND AND AUSTRALIA

Hiking the Overland Track

NORTH AMERICA

Hiking and Cycling the California Missions Trail
The John Muir Trail
The Pacific Crest Trail

SOUTH AMERICA

Aconcagua and the Southern Andes
Hiking and Biking Peru's Inca Trails
Trekking in Torres del Paine

SCANDINAVIA, ICELAND AND GREENLAND

Hiking in Norway – South
Trekking in Greenland – The Arctic Circle Trail
Trekking the Kungsleden
Walking and Trekking in Iceland

SLOVENIA, CROATIA, SERBIA, MONTENEGRO AND ALBANIA

Hiking Slovenia's Juliana Trail
Mountain Biking in Slovenia
The Islands of Croatia
The Julian Alps of Slovenia
The Mountains of Montenegro
The Peaks of the Balkans Trail
The Slovene Mountain Trail
Walking in Slovenia: The Karavanke
Walks and Treks in Croatia

SPAIN AND PORTUGAL

Camino de Santiago: Camino Frances
Coastal Walks in Andalucia
Costa Blanca Mountain Adventures
Cycling the Camino de Santiago
Cycling the Ruta Via de la Plata
Mountain Walking in Mallorca
Mountain Walking in Southern Catalunya
Portugal's Rota Vicentina
Spain's Sendero Historico: The GR1
The Andalucian Coast to Coast Walk
The Camino del Norte and Camino Primitivo
The Camino Ingles and Ruta do Mar
The Camino Portugues
The Mountains of Nerja
The Mountains of Ronda and Grazalema
The Sierras of Extremadura
Trekking in Mallorca
Trekking in the Canary Islands
Trekking the GR7 in Andalucia
Walking and Trekking in the Sierra Nevada
Walking in Andalucia
Walking in Catalunya – Barcelona
Walking in Catalunya – Girona Pyrenees
Walking in Portugal
Walking in the Algarve
Walking in the Picos de Europa
Walking La Via de la Plata and Camino Sanabres
Walking on Gran Canaria
Walking on La Gomera and El Hierro
Walking on La Palma
Walking on Lanzarote and Fuerteventura
Walking on Madeira
Walking on Tenerife
Walking on the Azores
Walking on the Costa Blanca
Walking the Camino dos Faros

SWITZERLAND

Switzerland's Jura Crest Trail
The Swiss Alps
Tour of the Jungfrau Region
Trekking the Swiss Via Alpina
Walking in the Bernese Oberland – Jungfrau region
Walking in the Engadine – Switzerland
Walking in the Valais
Walking in Ticino
Walking in Zermatt and Saas-Fee

CHINA, JAPAN AND ASIA

Hiking and Trekking in the Japan Alps and Mount Fuji
Hiking in Hong Kong
Japan's Kumano Kodo Pilgrimage
Trekking in Tajikistan

HIMALAYA

Annapurna
Everest: A Trekker's Guide
Trekking in Bhutan
Trekking in Ladakh
Trekking in the Himalaya

MOUNTAIN LITERATURE

8000 metres
A Walk in the Clouds
Abode of the Gods
Fifty Years of Adventure
The Pennine Way – the Path, the People, the Journey
Unjustifiable Risk?

TECHNIQUES

Fastpacking
Geocaching in the UK
Map and Compass
Outdoor Photography
The Mountain Hut Book

MINI GUIDES

Alpine Flowers
Navigation
Pocket First Aid and Wilderness Medicine
Snow